VGM Opportunities Series

OPPORTUNITIES IN
FUNERAL SERVICES
CAREERS

Terence J. Sacks

Foreword by
Joan D. Tomczak, Registrar
Stephanie J. Kann, Director
Worsham College of Mortuary Science

VGM Career Horizons
a division of *NTC Publishing Group*
Lincolnwood, Illinois USA

Cover Photo Credits:

All photos courtesy of San Francisco College of Mortuary Science, San Francisco, California

Library of Congress Cataloging-in-Publishing Data

Sacks, Terence J.
    Opportunities in funeral services careers / Terence J. Sacks.
        p.   cm.
    Includes bibliographical references (p.).
    ISBN 0-8442-4558-5 (alk. paper). — ISBN 0-8442-4559-3 (pbk. :
alk. paper)
    1. Undertakers and undertaking—Vocational guidance—United
States.   I. Title.
HD9999.U53U573   1997
363.7'5'02373—dc21   96-47295
                                                                 CIP

Published by VGM Career Horizons, a division of NTC Publishing Group
4255 West Touhy Avenue
Lincolnwood (Chicago), Illinois 60646-1975, U.S.A.
© 1997 by NTC Publishing Group. All rights reserved.
No part of this book may be reproduced, stored in a retrieval
system, or transmitted in any form or by any means,
electronic, mechanical, photocopying, recording or otherwise,
without the prior permission of NTC Publishing Group.
Manufactured in the United States of America.

7 8 9 0 VP 9 8 7 6 5 4 3 2 1

CONTENTS

ABOUT THE AUTHOR

Terry Sacks is an independent writer-editor with more than twenty-five years of experience in communications. During that period he has written dozens of news stories, magazine articles, and speeches. Sacks's articles have appeared in such publications as *Hospitals* and *Chicago Medicine.*

Sacks, a graduate of Northwestern University's Medill School of Journalism, has strong credentials in health- and medical-related topics. For three years, from 1970 through 1973, he was director of communications for the Chicago Medical Society, the local professional group for physicians in Chicago and Cook County. He has also held positions in communications for the American Osteopathic Association, the American Association of Dental Schools, and for several hospitals in Chicago.

Sacks is currently on the journalism faculty of Columbia College in Chicago, where he teaches "Introduction to the Mass Media." At Columbia he has also taught courses in news reporting, feature writing, editing company publications, and the history of journalism.

For the past ten years, Sacks has headed his own writing and communications firm, Terence J. Sacks Associates. He is active in the Independent Writers of Chicago (where he is also on the board), the American Medical Writers Association, and the Publicity Club of Chicago.

FOREWORD

In describing the role of funeral service professionals, what comes to mind is that they are the angels on earth. The funeral director serves as a guardian, guiding the family through the arrangements and service. Although the focus of the funeral is on the deceased, the funeral is intended for the living, and it provides the following benefits:

- Celebrates the life that was lived
- Allows family and friends to remember and honor their loved one at a time when it's needed most
- Encourages the expression of feelings and emotions
- Re-emphasizes the value of religion through ceremonies and rituals
- Provides closure for the bereaved
- Confirms the reality and finality of the death
- Encourages the bereaved to realize the pain of their loss and express those thoughts and feelings
- Assists the bereaved to cope with their grief and move forward with their lives

Funeral service professionals are among the outstanding members of their communities, setting the standards for moral and ethical behavior in their social as well as professional lives. The funeral director must demonstrate such qualities as competence, dedication, commitment, respect, sensitivity, and empathy. In today's changing world of computerization and technology, funeral service is expanding to meet the needs unique to each family, while remaining dedicated to the values and traditions of our society.

Joan D. Tomczak, Registrar
Stephanie J. Kann, Director
Worsham College of Mortuary Science

CHAPTER 1

A LOOK AT THE PROFESSION

Judy Claremont (not her real name) sits at a huge semicircular desk under an enormous crystal chandelier. Where you might ordinarily expect to see a wooden or plastic nameplate is a granite rock upon which her name is engraved.

Mirrors are to be seen throughout the handsome room, which is decorated in soothing beige leather and chrome steel chairs and benches.

Judy, you see, is a funeral director, and her office occupies a prominent spot in the funeral home that her father established in a large New England town some forty-eight years ago. She remembers how depressing and dreary she found the home as a child, and when the opportunity to redo the home arose, after it had been burnt to the ground, she did it up to suit her taste in bright, modern decor.

While she sat at her desk a call came in. Judy's voice was warm and soothing as she spoke. "Hi, Betty," she said, pausing for an answer. "Don't worry...that's okay...we'll take care of everything."

"I think you did the right thing. Your Dad was buried there, too."

"Whatever makes you comfortable, that's what we'll do."

"I understand that, certainly. Whatever you want, that's what we'll do."

"Don't worry—if you want donations instead of flowers we'll make that known."

"And remember, I'm as close as the phone if you need me. We'll see you tomorrow at nine to discuss the arrangements."

THE CHALLENGES OF THE PROFESSION

There's nothing as final as death, and for the survivors, death can be quite a nightmare as they struggle to get on with their lives while grieving the loss of a loved one.

It is in this very difficult place—somewhere between the finality of death and the need to carry on with the living—that the funeral director comes into the picture. Besides providing a shoulder to cry on, he or she helps the family and friends struggle through the reams of paperwork and administrative and clerical tasks that must be completed. A death certificate has to be prepared and copies sent to the Veterans Administration, Social Security Administration, and other government agencies so that the widow and/or children can begin to collect survivors' pensions, if any.

Funeral directors are by background and experience uniquely able to handle the myriad details—some assigned by law and others by custom and practice—that require attention when death occurs. Some tasks are simply administrative and logistical in nature, such as placing orders for caskets, making certain that a lot for burial is ready, ordering the vault that is placed in the burial site and into which the casket is lowered before burial, for instance.

But most important is the task that calls for involvement with the bereaved family, and this includes sensitive, caring intervention in their personal lives.

To get some idea of the tasks that must be handled by the funeral director when death occurs, consider this. Once the family has selected the funeral director, he or she handles various tasks, usually in this order, but with some variation.

- arranges for the removal of the body from the hospital, nursing home, or other place of death to the funeral home
- obtains information for the death certificate and the newspaper obituary notice
- completes and files the death certificate

Following consultation with the family and/or other survivors, the funeral director then completes arrangements for the funeral service in accordance with the requirements of the law and the family's wishes. This covers such things as:

- place and time of services
- clergyman or other persons who will officiate and take part in the service
- type of final disposition—burial, cremation, or entombment
- casket and outer burial container (vault) according to the family's desires
- music, notification of pallbearers, prayerbooks, instructions on how to get to the cemetery, and so forth

Once the service has been completed, the funeral director helps the family in filing all required claims for social security, veteran's insurance and union and company benefits, and insurance.

But perhaps the funeral director's greatest service to the family and to the mourners is to serve as counselor. Families often turn to you as the funeral director as their first and last source of information. And though you may not be able to handle any deep-seated problems in handling grief, you can and do provide guidance in obtaining the professional care they may need.

Families often expect you to have all of the answers, solve all of the problems, and meet all of the financial, psychological, and physical needs. Obviously this is impossible, but as funeral director you can at least refer them to where they can get the kinds of assistance they seek.

Outside of the immediate concerns on your time, skills, and energy, you must take on an active role as caregiver outside the funeral home. Most likely you will become involved with skilled nursing and long-term care facilities; with hospices and the hospice movement; and with community outreach groups such as Compassionate Friends, Widow to Widow, and other volunteer organizations.

Obviously, you will want to become familiar with clergymen of all of the major denominations as well as physicians, nurses, and other personnel of hospitals and nursing homes in your community. Often their goodwill and friendship can be invaluable as sources of referral. You also will want to be active in religious and community groups such as Lions, Kiwanis, Rotary, and other service clubs, as well as your church or temple organizations. Here, again, such exposure is critical to your success.

Obviously the demands on your time and energy will be ferocious. Funeral service, as work in a funeral home is called, is not a nine to five job. Calls come in at all times, day and night. In the early days of your service as a funeral director, you can expect to work long hours and for relatively modest pay.

In larger cities, and especially so in smaller communities, you will be on call twenty-four hours a day. You may be planning to be with your family at Thanksgiving or Christmas time, but if a call comes in and you are on duty, you must put aside your plans and get to the funeral home at the first opportunity to be of service to the grieving family.

Such constant demands on your attention and energy can take their toll on your family relations, especially if you are married and have children. This is particularly true in the smaller community, where the funeral director may be on call at all times, with no one to spell him or her. Often plans to go on vacation or to sit in on some family function—a dinner, a wedding anniversary, or other event—go up in smoke when a call comes in. Funeral service is a rough business, especially when you're first starting out. Will you be equal to the demands imposed upon you as a funeral director?

But wait, is this all that you should be concerned about in this career? Not quite, because in addition to the long hours, there are other considerations. For one, there are the hazards associated with working with formaldehyde and other toxic chemicals. Despite the fact that the preparation rooms where the dead are embalmed are well-ventilated, there is always the possibility of ingesting potentially dangerous and cancer causing fumes.

And if you are not careful or are improperly garbed, there is the potential of spilling some hazardous chemicals on any exposed area of your body—face, hands, nose, and even your eyes. True, these hazards are quite slim if you are properly attired, but they are, nevertheless, there and a factor to consider.

In recent years, there is also the exposure to AIDS and other infectious diseases—such as pneumonia or hepatitis– that may be present in the dead person. Although the chance of contracting a disease is there, it is almost nil if you take proper precautions and are properly outfitted—with mask, gown, gloves and boots, as well as goggles.

There is also the fact that you will be working with all kinds of bodies—victims of gunshot wounds, accidents, stabbings, and other causes—and in rare cases, portions of their faces and their limbs may be missing. Can you withstand the demands of working under such circumstances? If you are truly dedicated to the profession, it will make no difference how you go about your work. It is all part of the business, as the expression goes, and something that you will have to be able to handle early on in this career.

THE ADVANTAGES OF THE PROFESSION

But is that all there is to funeral service? No, not by any means. There are also many pluses to the career that far outweigh the negatives. For one, funeral service has been rated by many familiar with careers as one of the top careers of all. For instance, in a recent study funeral service was ranked the top managerial job by Cognetics, a Massachusetts research firm.

And to anyone familiar with the profession this is no surprise. For instance the *Washington Post* recently quoted George Rowles, director of the Arlington Funeral Home, near Washington, D.C., as saying: "It's one business where you can't have a recession. Though money may be tight, people still die, and they still have a service."

Then, too, the funeral service industry is very stable. According to Rowles in the *Post* article: "I've never heard of a funeral home going out of business, at least not one of the established ones."

Despite the movement and change in modern life, funeral homes continue to exist. The average home has been in the community, for the most part in the same location, for more than forty years, and homes with a history of one hundred or more years are not exceptional. And in many homes, the same family has been in charge for six and even seven generations.

The pay, while relatively modest, is not bad either. According to a 1995 salary survey of the National Funeral Directors Association, funeral directors/embalmers in the smallest category of funeral homes surveyed (those doing fewer than one hundred services a year) received $26,000 a year, while those employed in the larger homes (those performing two hundred or more services a year) earned $34,000.

And the top reported salaries of all—those in the owner/manager category—averaged $56,382 per year. Added to a bonus, which in 1994 averaged $10,963, this brought total earnings for the owner/manager to $67,345.

Nor does this include benefits, which are excellent, for the most part, with most firms providing paid vacations, medical insurance, profit sharing, pension programs, and sick leave.

But this completely overlooks what is undoubtedly the key feature of funeral service, and the factor that possibly explains more than anything else why funeral directors are willing to put up with the long hours, occupational hazards, and other negatives—the chance to be of real service to families when they are especially vulnerable and confused.

As Mindy Botbol, a student at Worsham School of Mortuary Science near Chicago, put it: "There was this situation where I was meeting with one of the funeral directors to make a prearrangement for this woman, and I sat in on the arrangements and she told me: 'You know, Mindy, I don't know if you noticed that I kept staring into your eyes. I was looking at you for the strength you gave me that I needed.' Nothing in the world is more worthwhile than to have someone tell you that."

Perhaps that is why funeral directors tend to stay on the job for years, with the average tenured service at a funeral home ten years or more.

WHAT IT TAKES TO SUCCEED

So how can you tell if you have what it takes to succeed in this profession? Here are a few simple questions you can ask yourself.

Do you want to serve others, especially those who may be unable to meet their own needs?

Can you accept that people show their grief in unique ways—some quietly and others more emotionally?

Are you tolerant of the ways in which people of different faiths and beliefs express their feelings and practice their religion?

Are you sensitive to the inherent dignity of every human being? That you can not discriminate by race, ethnic group, or age when a person dies?

Can you accept a profession that demands round-the-clock sensitivity to the needs and wishes of those in mourning?

Aside from these few simple questions, you should be attempting right now, while you are still in school, to judge your suitability for this career.

For one, visit a college of mortuary science. If possible, try to sit in on a class or two to get an idea of what the course is like.

Talk to the school director or registrar. Get some idea of what the curriculum is like and what they are looking for in their students. Check on college requirements—total number of credits required as well as any special courses in chemistry, anatomy, and so forth.

If possible, talk to some students. Get their slant on the mortuary college—its strong points as well as the negatives. Sometimes you can get a better idea of what the school has to offer in this manner than in any other way.

And while you are scouting around, check with the funeral home in your area to see if you can obtain any part-time employment. Even a job trimming bushes or mowing the lawn can help inasmuch as you get exposure to the industry.

At the very least talk to some funeral directors in your community. Chances are they will be glad to talk to you. See if they will take you through the funeral home to see where the various phases of the work are performed, especially the preparation room, where the dead are embalmed.

Check out opportunities for leadership in your school. Join student government and become active in such school service clubs as Key Club and Leo Club.

Take any science courses that you can, especially those in chemistry, microbiology, and anatomy. Also take writing and speech courses, since the work requires good verbal and writing abilities.

So what precisely does it take to succeed in funeral service? Says one who should know, Joan Tomczak, long-time owner and registrar of Worsham College of Mortuary Science near Chicago: "You should first of all be sensitive to the needs of people who are very vulnerable—someone who respects death and the body they are working with . . . who treats the dead in a caring way as shown by how they treat them and care for them. Treat them as you would if the family were alongside you in the room where you are preparing the body."

You also need emotional stability. "Families don't need someone to sit down and cry with them," is the way Ms. Tomczak puts it. "They need someone with strength, who is empathetic with their needs."

You also need to be honest and ethical in your dealings with the public, ready to serve them in their various needs. And above all, she says, you should never become so hardened or calloused that you cannot feel for people in their time of grief. "If you do not feel for them," says Ms. Tomczak, "you should not be in this business."

Just two further points in closing. Vanderlyn M. Pine in his excellent book, *Caretaker for the Dead: The American Funeral Director*, notes two other possible points of frustration and confusion that you should be aware of.

The first is that since most people in our society regard death and dying as a negative—something to be avoided at all possible cost—people tend to look upon funeral directors with some distaste and abhorrence. This is much less of a problem today than it has been in the past, but let's face it, there is still a certain stigma attached to the profession by many people, and people associated with the profession will quickly become aware of this, if they are not already aware of it. Most professionals know that such feelings are due primarily to ignorance and fear, and they overlook any negative vibrations that they may encounter in the course of their work. In some cases people may shun you, but more likely you will encounter senseless and even cruel jokes about the profession that people foolishly believe will help to break the ice. Your best bet is simply to ignore these sad attempts at humor as best as you can. Nevertheless this is something that you should be aware of, for it is a very real consideration.

Second, many Protestant ministers tend to regard funeral directors with some distaste since funeral directors are open to all religions and faiths in the conduct of their profession, and according to Pine, such impartiality or openness on the part of the funeral director can be construed by some ministers to mean that their denomination is relegated to a secondary role. This latter interpretation is reported for what it's worth and is subject to debate.

So there you have it, a look at the pros and cons of funeral service with no effort to gloss over the negatives or emphasize the positives. In the chapters to come we will look at other aspects of the profession that you should understand if you are serious about considering a career as a funeral director.

Chapter 2 reviews the history of funeral service from ancient times through the present day, paying special attention to some of the trends that are affecting the funeral industry today. Chapter 3 looks at the duties and responsibilities of the funeral director. Chapter 4 discusses the requirements for licensure—admission to mortuary college, apprenticeship requirements, and licensure examinations. Chapter 5 takes a look at the demographics of the profession and the earnings possible. Chapter 6 discusses the job outlook of the profession. And Chapter 7 offers some conversations with those in the industry, including students, apprentices, funeral directors, and educators.

CHAPTER 2

FUNERAL SERVICE: THEN AND NOW

EARLY FUNERAL PRACTICES

Since the beginning of time, mankind has developed customs to dispose of the dead, comfort the living, and express grief. Although the manner of disposing of the dead may vary considerably from one civilization to another, nearly all societies believe that human beings survive death in one form or another.

In some religions death merely symbolizes a passage from one life to another, as is the case in Hinduism. And the method of disposing of the dead bodies varies drastically from interment in pyramids or tombs to cremation to burning pyres and being sunk beneath ocean waves to burial in the ground as is true of our society. Although disposition of the body varies, there are many common elements found in societies throughout the world: public announcements of the death, preparation of the body, religious ceremonies or other services, processions to the cemetery or burial ground, a burial or some other form of disposal, and finally a mourning period.

While preparation of the body varies among peoples, typically it is laid out and washed. Sometimes it is painted and anointed with spices and oils. In most societies it is then dressed in special garments or wrapped in a cloth called a shroud. Most often the corpse is placed in a coffin, also known as a casket, or other container.

In many societies, an all-night watch is held in the belief that in so doing, the watch or wake comforts the dead and protects the body from evil spirits. In the past, the watch also was held to watch for possible signs of life.

In the United States and Canada, where most bodies are kept for several days before burial, cremation, or entombment, funeral directors preserve the body through a process known as embalmment. Here the embalmer removes the blood and injects a chemical solution into the corpse to prevent decay. During the period immediately preceding the funeral, and in many cases in the days to follow, relatives and friends may come to view the body. In the United States and Canada, embalming is not required, and indeed it is frowned upon by orthodox Jews, who believe that the body must not be mutilated. Such beliefs also serve to prohibit cremation and autopsies of the body among religious Jews.

Ordinarily funeral services may include prayers, choral music, hymns and other music, and speeches or eulogies that recall and praise the dead person. In this country, funerals are held primarily at the funeral home, with the body in many cases on display. Following the service, a special vehicle known as a hearse carries it in a procession to the cemetery or crematory, where after a brief ceremony, the body is either buried or cremated.

In many cases, the mourners return with the grieving family to their home or other location for refreshments and prayer.

Among Christians, Jews, and Muslims, burial is still the most common means of disposal, under the belief that the dead will rise again; thus like a seed, it is placed in earth awaiting rebirth.

Cremation, practiced commonly among Buddhists and Hindus, is still relatively uncommon in this country, although it is on the rise. Orthodox Jews and some Protestants oppose this practice in the belief that the body is the dwelling place of the soul and should not be destroyed. Even so, cremation is on the rise in both the United States and Canada and currently accounts for nearly 20 percent of the interments in this country.

But there are many other ways various societies dispose of their dead. The Sioux Indians, for instance, place their dead on high platforms. Some aborigines, the original inhabitants of Australia, leave their dead in trees. And in Tibet, bodies are immersed in the water. In India a religious sect, the Parsis, take their dead to special enclosures known as towers of silence, where birds pick the corpses clean. Parsis believe that earth and fire are sacred and must not be defiled by burying or burning a corpse.

Even with these differences in disposing of the remains, mourning is common after death. Often the mourners are required to refrain from any form of entertainment and are restricted in what foods they can eat. Orthodox Jews customarily tear their clothing as an expression of grief, or wear tattered black ribbons in place of such rending of clothing. And until the 1940s in this country and in Europe, people wore black armbands and hung funeral wreaths on their doors while in mourning.

In some societies, death is regarded as a time of uncleanliness that contaminates the survivors and makes them taboo (set aside as cursed or sacred).

But the evolution of funeral customs in handling the disposal of the body and in mourning has occurred over thousands of years almost since the beginning of history. For instance, the ancient Egyptians practiced a very intricate and elaborate system of care for the dead, which was built upon a very extensive division of labor. Undertakers and embalming specialists cared for the preparation of the dead and carried out many of the funeral arrangements. It was the Egyptians' belief that the dead must be preserved by embalming because after death the soul leaves the body to travel through time, eventually returning to reinhabit the dead body

Embalming, which was practiced by the ancient Egyptians as early as 4000 B.C., was a highly skilled art. They believed that a mummy, or preserved body, was necessary for the survival of the soul or spirit. The process varied according to the deceased's wealth or prominence, but in most cases, the embalmer first soaked the body in a soda solution and then filled the body cavity with oils, spices, and resins. Pitch and tar, which were commonly used for preservation, gave the mummies a black appearance.

In 1881, archaeologists discovered the 3,200-year-old mummy of the Egyptian King, Ramses II, believed to have been Pharoah at the time of Moses.

In ancient Greece, where embalming was not practiced, preparation of the dead was left to the family. Perfumes and spices were commonly used to mask the odor of decaying flesh. Flowers for the dead were provided by family and friends. The Greeks were among those who viewed the dead body largely to make certain that death had actually occurred and that the body had not been molested. Later, since the Greeks believed that flames set the soul free, cremation was often practiced. But to these ancient Greeks, death was widely regarded as a personal matter with certain experienced family members serving as funeral experts.

The funeral practices of ancient Rome have had a direct bearing on those of today. Both burial and cremation were practiced at various times; in either case, the body was placed on display for viewing by the public prior to disposition. The rich were cared for by a professional undertaker, known as a *libitinarian,* whose work was fairly well defined. It was the libitinarian who handled anointing and embalming, supplied professional mourners and mourning garments, and arranged for services aimed at relieving the grief of the mourners. In addition, he handled the details of the funeral procession.

Since the ancient Jews believed that man was composed of two elements—flesh and breath—they believed that flesh returned to dust while the breath persisted. Therefore, cremation was abhorrent and prohibited, and burial with or without a coffin was practiced.

The Jewish practice of washing of the dead and burial on the evening of the day of the death were carried out largely by experienced family members. Once the dead were prepared, professional mourners were often used during the funeral itself.

Early Christian funeral practices were simple and unpretentious. Friends and relatives customarily followed the long-standing Jewish custom of watching or *waking* the dead, a practice arising primarily out of fear of burying a live person. Early Christians believed, as is still true today, that death is not an end in itself but merely a transition from life in this world to the afterworld.

From about the fourth century A.D., following the church's institution of feast days to commemorate the anniversaries of the death of martyrs, the Christian funeral evolved into a more complex ceremony as part of a developing society. While most of the early Christians funeral activities were performed by the family of the dead, this was done usually under the direction of the clergy.

In time the simple burial practices of the early Christians gave way to more ceremonious practices with the development of the church.

In the Middle Ages, embalming practices of Christians included removing some body organs, washing the body with either alcohol or fragrant oils, chemically drying and preserving the flesh, wrapping the body in layers of cloth sealed with tar or oak sap, and mummification, similar to that performed by the Egyptians.

Modern embalming stems from about 1700 when a Dutch anatomist, Frederick Ruysch, developed a formula that when injected into the arteries would preserve a lifelike appearance in the corpse. Today, of course, embalmers remove body fluids and inject a chemical compound containing formaldehyde, mercuric chloride, zinc chloride, and alcohol.

Even earlier, Leonardo Da Vinci, the great Italian painter and anatomist, developed a system of venous injection of the cadaver to allow him to make his famous anatomical plates. This served as a prototype for early medical embalmers to follow. By the end of the seventeenth century, embalming was commonly practiced to preserve the dead for anatomical dissection. Thus embalming developed as a medical practice with little association to funeral practices as we know them.

And during this period, the late seventeenth century, English tradesmen, primarily occupied as livery stable owners, carpenters, and cabinetmakers, took on some of the undertaking tasks as the work became more defined and specialized.

By the eighteenth century, the English funeral had evolved into a full-fledged ceremony with mutes, mourners, and livery gathered to provide the proper atmosphere of gloom and mourning for the deceased.

FUNERAL PRACTICES IN AMERICA

Early colonists accepted death as natural and saw no reason to disguise cemeteries because they believed that life and death were two sides of the same coin. Funeral services were simple and mourners were active participants accompanying the coffin to the grave and piling dirt on the grave. To enhance the communal nature of the process, personal items such as hats, rings, scarfs, gloves, and purses often were given away as a tribute to the dead.

Undertaking gradually evolved by taking over certain tasks formerly handled primarily by cabinetmakers, carpenters, or family members. As certain members of the community became experienced in caring for the dead, some began to offer their services to others in the town, and by the end of the eighteenth century, the laying out of the dead had become a specialty, unique unto itself.

During the nineteenth century, the American undertaker began to combine certain functions formerly scattered among several trades. And with the trend toward development of large cities, families became increasingly unable to handle the laying out of the dead themselves.

Continuing on previous traditions, funerals in the nineteenth century were largely gloomy affairs, according to the wishes of the bereaved. Increasingly the public began to feel the need to provide a more beautiful setting for funerals, and undertakers began to be called increasingly to the home immediately after the death of a loved one. Working primarily out of the home, they directed the funeral in the presence of and with the cooperation of the dead person's family. Often embalming was carried out in the home, and embalmers attempted to restore the face of the dead with liquid tints developed by embalming fluid companies.

Contributing greatly to the growth of the funeral service industry and embalming was the Civil War, in which large numbers of soldiers were killed far from their homes. To facilitate transporting bodies back home, embalmers emerged in increasing number around Civil War battlefields. And the assassination of President Lincoln and subsequent display of Lincoln's body in the funeral procession from Washington, D.C., to the President's home in Springfield, made people even more aware of embalming.

By the end of the nineteenth century, as people became more concerned about burial and cremation permits, states began to enact licensing laws regulating the practice of embalming and the filing of death certificates.

Funeral services were normally conducted in the deceased's home. The undertaker would bring all supplies and equipment to the home and set them up in the living room or parlor, hence the name funeral parlor. A basket of flowers was hung on the front door, replacing a crepe badge used earlier to mark the bereaved's home. Usually religious services were conducted either at the home or in church with the funeral procession to the cemetery following. There remained one further important task: the removal of all signs of a funeral while the home was vacant for the funeral procession, a job the funeral director handled.

About this time, the end of the nineteenth century, funeral homes began to appear in certain cities because of the need for a place for funeral equipment. And in smaller towns, undertakers began to use the rear rooms of stores, their own barns, or their living rooms to provide a place for the funeral for those families whose home was no longer appropriate for laying out of the dead. In this homelike setting, the undertaker, as he was called, supplied the coffin, robes, pillows, and crucifixes, and he began to assume responsibility for the entire funeral service.

At this time, several factors contributed to the development of this new occupation. First, the mobility of Americans and the decline of the extended family led to the emergence of smaller homes, which were inadequate to serve as places where families could gather to mourn the death of their loved ones. New funeral parlors were built expressly for the purpose of serving the dead and the bereaved families.

And as embalming became more sophisticated, it became increasingly difficult to bring the required equipment into private homes. Embalming more and more became the responsibility of the newly developed funeral parlors.

Finally, the problems connected with gathering mourners for funeral services at the church, added to the trend to have separate funeral homes for funeral ceremonies. This combination of a large home with a chapel-like appearance, attached to a special laboratory led to today's modern funeral home. As a result, the funeral director came to be regarded as much more than a provider of goods and equipment; he was viewed as someone with the managerial skills as well as the background and experience necessary to handle the special needs of families during their time of mourning.

Today funeral homes are to be found all over the country, in small, rural communities to large, metropolitan areas. According to the National Funeral Directors Association (NFDA), in 1996, 6 percent of all funeral homes were located in large cities (those of from 100,000 to more than a million in population); 15.8 percent of all funeral homes were located in cities of 25,000 to 100,000; 29.1 percent were in smaller cities of 2,500 to 25,000, and the vast majority of the homes, 49.3 percent, were located in communities of fewer than 2,500.

According to the 1996 NFDA survey, the average home was in business more than fifty-seven years, was a corporation, and was independently owned and operated. In addition, the average funeral director owned 1.5 facilities, was college educated (40 percent), or had an associate degree (usually awarded after two years of college). A few funeral directors owned cemeteries (6.4 percent) and crematories (6.2 percent). The final point brought out in the survey was that the overwhelming preponderance of funeral directors (estimated at more than 95 percent) were men. However, women are starting to make their mark in this profession and can be expected to be much more of a factor in the industry in years to come.

To see how the American funeral industry compares with that abroad, let's look at funeral service in three widely separate countries—countries separated not only by geography, but by custom and religion.

The first of these is Great Britain. In Britain economic factors determine to a great extent the kind of funeral service held. Families with more modest means may select a carpenter shop with an undertaking business as a sideline, while wealthier people may deal primarily with a firm that is exclusively a funeral home.

The service also is affected by geography. In the south, for instance, the service ends at the grave, while in the north of Britain, the funeral director will arrange for high tea for all mourners at the conclusion of the cemetery service.

In either case, the dead body is cared for at the place of death, either by a nurse or a funeral director. Embalming, which is not legally required, is optional. Even so, bodies that are embalmed are treated only to hold up to the day of the funeral, and there is no attempt to create a lifelike appearance in the dead. Although the use of embalming is growing, with some firms reporting the embalming of 80 to 90 percent of the dead, only an estimated 7 to 10 percent of all bodies receive temporary embalming, primarily in private homes.

The British tend to prefer not to view the body. Although such viewing takes place primarily in the home, the trend is increasingly to utilize the funeral home for this purpose and to arrange for complete funerals, including the casket, embalming, viewing, and other services.

Basically there are two types of funeral homes. The more traditional homes are more conservative in their funeral arrangements, for example, working out of the place of death.

However, recently there has been a trend toward cooperative funeral establishments, which are run by voting members. In these coops, the trend has been more to holding funerals in the funeral homes and practicing embalmment and viewing of the dead by friends and relatives.

In Japan, care of the dead is based primarily on where the death occurs: in rural villages or in large, urban centers.

In the villages, funerals are regulated largely by the village head, and the entire village works as a team to provide all the required equipment, services, and labor. Relatives of the deceased are contacted and they customarily gather in the home of the deceased to conduct the funeral ceremonies. Disposition is handled by distant relatives and friends who place the body in a wooden coffin. The rites are, therefore, highly personalized.

In urban centers, the services are more Westernized in approach. Funeral establishments are owned either privately or by municipal or national governments. Since custom says that the immediate family is too upset by death to be involved directly, arrangements are handled largely by distant relatives and friends.

Although there is little embalming or public viewing of the dead, the immediate family does gather to view the deceased in the coffin—but only the face, which is painted white, is visible. And friends and relatives call to express their condolences. Funerals are held either at the home of the deceased or at their temple.

Funeral directors primarily provide funeral equipment, which they deliver to the place where the funeral is to be held, and supply transportation. Afterwards, the deceased is cremated. The following day, the family returns to the crematory to collect the ashes and bones of the deceased, which are then buried. Usually this final disposition of the remains is performed with an elaborate ceremony.

In Russia, funeral practices have evolved over the past seventy or so years. Following the Russian Revolution of 1917, government regulations called for the immediate, unceremonial interment of the body. But over the past half century or so, the government has become much more flexible and has taken into account the wishes of the bereaved family.

Recently, the Soviet government has been granting funds to the bereaved family for the funeral. All necessary equipment can be obtained at state-operated funeral stores, which have fixed prices for all merchandise and equipment including coffins, hearses, and so forth.

Arrangements are largely made by the family of the deceased, and embalming is optional and done by medically trained specialists. Ordinarily viewing of the dead is done either at the home of the deceased or in the hospital where the death occurred. Typically this is followed by a funeral service within forty-eight hours after the viewing.

From this, it is apparent that funeral service as we know it in this country is unique to America, and while there are some similarities in the practices of all three countries, they vary considerably from funeral service in this country.

CHAPTER 3

WHAT DO FUNERAL DIRECTORS DO?

Having seen, in Chapter 2, how funeral service evolved in this country, let us take a more detailed look in this chapter at what funeral directors do. In general their duties fall into several categories: external, or public activities; behind-the-scenes activities; and activities outside of the funeral home.

First a detailed look at the external activities, or those involving either the mourners or the public in general.

PUBLIC ACTIVITIES

Many homes prefer to answer calls in person, because every call that comes in is a potential notice of a death in the family. Most homes, therefore, staff their offices around the clock, so that no person who has suffered the death of a loved one need deal with an answering service or a telephone recorder. This creates a more personalized, caring atmosphere.

At this point, it is necessary to reassure the person calling that his or her needs are paramount and that all possible efforts will be extended to make sure that those needs are met.

Ordinarily, the details required to complete the death certificate and the funeral arrangements are left for the following day, when the funeral director will be able to speak to the mourners face to face. At this point your primary concern is to determine where the death occurred so that arrangements can be made to remove the body and to transport it to the funeral home. And you want to be seen as concerned, knowledgeable, and anxious to be of help.

The completion of this all-important first call sets in motion a flurry of activities that occur primarily behind the scenes, such as the transporting, embalming, and laying out of the body, all of which are described below in the section on nonpublic activities.

Following the first call and some time after the removal of the body from the place of death, you should sit down with the family or loved ones to plan the funeral, or to make the arrangements, as it is called.

Quite often the family will use you as a sounding board to voice their concerns about death and dying and how this will affect them and their children. It is important that you as funeral director hear them out and show your sympathy, understanding, and concern for all of their problems and questions.

During this interview, it is important that you explain as much as possible about the various aspects of the funeral. This is the time to try to allay the family's concerns and fears by answering their questions as fully as you can. Such questions might include:

Will we have a chance to look at the body?

When can we see our loved one?

Are visiting hours customary, and if so, when is it customary to have them?

Should we bring the children with us to the funeral?

What should we do when people come to the chapel? Where should we be?

What about our social security checks, joint bank accounts?

What should we do about our insurance policy?

What cemetery can we buy a plot in?

Although some of these questions may seem trivial to you, to the bereaved they are all important, and you should be able to answer them directly. If not, you should be able to refer the family to a source where they can get this information.

An important part of making arrangements is selecting the date, time, and place for the funeral service. In Jewish funerals, services are usually scheduled within twenty-four hours of the death. It is therefore not required that the deceased be embalmed, but for sanitary and cosmetic purposes, embalming is increasingly the choice among Jewish families as well.

Other key questions that must be answered are the names of the officiating clergy, cantor, and any others to be associated with the service.

Increasingly the trend in funeral services is to have family members, friends, and business associates of the deceased give eulogies, or short talks, in praise of the deceased. Other questions requiring answers include: Will there be music? Are flowers allowed? Do mourners prefer donations instead of flowers?

In most cases you will attempt to schedule services to fit the family's convenience—either the morning or afternoon of the day of their choice, but this of course is subject to the availability of the chapel for that particular day and time.

One of the most crucial parts of arranging the funeral concerns the selection of the coffin, or casket, as funeral directors call it. Here it is part of your job as funeral director to explain to the family the differences in caskets if this information is requested.

Since the selection of the casket is one of the big ticket costs of the funeral, it is important that you assist the family in selecting a casket that is within their means. This can be quite a chore with the number of caskets on display ranging from twelve to more than thirty-six and the cost from a few hundred dollars to many thousands of dollars.

As might be expected, most purchases fall into the middle price range. Here you also gather information for the funeral service itself—details on what to include in the obituary notice and in which newspapers to put it, who to select for pallbearers, and so forth.

Once the arrangements have been made and the body has been prepared, the next order of business is arranging for visitation, the period during which the family, friends, and business associates of the deceased come to pay their respects. It is also often referred to as the *wake,* or viewing or visiting hours.

Ordinarily the first viewing is done by the immediate members of the family. Due to the efforts of the funeral home to restore the deceased to as lifelike an appearance as possible, this ordinarily produces a positive reaction. But it can be a very emotionally exhausting time, since this is the family's first look at the deceased.

Often your concern with the appearance of the deceased can enhance your professionalism in the eyes of the family and help them to come to grips with the death of their loved one.

At some funeral homes you may be called on to act as doorman, supervisor, confidant, and friend, but at all times your primary responsibility is to the mourners. Visitation is also a time for becoming acquainted with family members and other friends, and such exposure can boost your image as a professional and concerned caregiver.

On the night prior to the funeral service, in many funeral homes, you will visit the family to make sure that everything is being handled satisfactorily. This is a good time to review such details as the cemetery to be used, the time of the service, the names of the pallbearers, the officiating clergy, and any other aspects of the service to make sure that your records are accurate. Such a call also can serve as a reminder of your concern and will help to enhance your status as a caring and concerned professional.

As to the funeral itself, it can occur at the funeral home, at the home of the deceased, in a church or temple, in a public building, or at the cemetery.

The service customarily includes prayers, hymns, and other music. Eulogies, which recall and praise the dead person, are also commonly a part of the service, with the embalmed body on display, the casket open or closed as the family wishes. Ordinarily, a special vehicle known as a hearse carries the deceased to the cemetery, where there may be a final brief ceremony, and the body is either buried, entombed (placed in a tomb above ground), or, as is increasingly common these days, cremated. After the funeral the mourners commonly return to their home and partake of food. Later, perhaps a year after the service is held, a tombstone or other monument is installed to mark the place of burial and to some extent to record the dead person's life.

Burial is the most common method of disposal in this country and in other countries of the Western world and in Muslim countries. But cremation, currently estimated to account for 10 percent of all disposals, is the preferred method in Hindu and Buddhist countries. But even where cremation is selected for disposal of the remains, an urn or casket is quite commonly used to hold the ashes. In other cases, the ashes are scattered over water, or in the air.

In a growing number of funeral ceremonies, funeral rites at the funeral home are omitted in favor of a brief, graveside ceremony.

So much for the funeral director's external or visible activities, those that the mourners and the public are party to. But is this all there is to funeral directing? Not by a long shot.

BEHIND-THE-SCENES ACTIVITIES

A good number of your responsibilities as a funeral director involve activities not ordinarily seen by the public. Such activities include removal of the body from the place of death, embalming, restorative measures to make the body appear as lifelike as possible, and placing of the body in the casket in a viewing room.

Removal of the body is ordinarily routine, but there can be unforeseen complications, for instance, when the body has been lying in a home for several days before the funeral home is notified. Under those conditions, the body is subject to deterioration and decay and removal can be quite unpleasant.

Ordinarily this is not a problem, as 90 percent of the removals are made from hospitals, nursing homes, and homes for senior citizens. If an autopsy is done, in cases where the circumstances of death are suspicious or unknown, there can be delays. Other delays can occur when the physician is not available to sign the death certificate, and the family insists that their family physician alone can sign.

Embalming is the next step of the procedure, and while embalming is required in cases where more than twenty-four hours have transpired between death and the time of services, or where death has been due to some infectious disease, for sanitizing purposes, it is not ordinarily required.

Embalming in general is aimed at keeping the body in a lifelike appearance. It retards decay and meets the requirements of some religions. It also facilitates shipment of the body and is required where the body must be held several days for a funeral.

Here there are several steps that you would ordinarily follow. First the body and hair are cleansed. Next an incision is made either at the base of the neck or in the groin to gain access to a major artery and vein. Then tubes are inserted into the artery or vein, and the artery is attached to a mechanical pump that injects a preservative and disinfectant solution into the body's vascular system, which is comprised of all of the veins and arteries.

The circulation of the chemical solution into the arterial network eventually forces the blood out of the draining tube. The final step is a process in which you remove the gases and liquids from the organs and introduce a disinfectant chemical into the body.

There are several very good reasons why the family or any layperson is not ordinarily allowed to view the embalming. For one, the embalming process often is complicated by such things as clots, aneurisms, and other blood blockages, and it is common practice to let the blood flow freely. This can be quite upsetting to those unaccustomed to the procedure. In addition, in a large funeral home several bodies may be in the process of being embalmed at the same time. Finally, the blood tends to drain from the head down to the lower limbs leaving the head an unnatural putty color, a sight hardly calculated to elicit joy from loved ones. Usually the entire embalming process lasts from about one to two hours.

In the next step you attempt to repair disfigured parts of the body and make the color and appearance of the face as lifelike as possible. To do this you work with wax, cotton, plaster of paris, and cosmetics.

In larger funeral homes there are funeral directors who do nothing but embalming and even restoration of the deceased through cosmetic facial restoration.

Finally, there is left only the placement of the dead person in the casket and the positioning of the deceased in the funeral chapel. Even here, as a funeral director, you are concerned with how the family and the visiting public will view the deceased. Placement of the casket and flowers in the chapel, and even the chair arrangement, can become an important part of the overall impression conveyed to the public and the deceased's loved ones.

Usually the casket is placed on a movable platform with the fully clad and restored body in it. The casket is then moved into the chapel for viewing until the time of the service.

Once the casket is placed, you attend to the general setting and to such details as making sure the deceased has clean eyeglasses, a lint-free suit, polished fingernails, and flowers positioned around the casket.

Also comprising a good part of your work is paperwork. As mentioned before, helping family members to fill out and file the proper forms for veterans benefits, insurance, Social Security benefits, and pension benefits are a part of your responsibilities.

Since a funeral home is a business, you are required to keep records on expenses, purchases, and services performed. You also are often called on to prepare and send bills for services rendered and for federal, state, and local tax forms.

ACTIVITIES OUTSIDE THE FUNERAL HOME

As a funeral director, you will almost have to participate in various community organizations, service clubs, church and temple groups, and so forth. In fact in many large funeral homes, where several directors are involved, one may join Kiwanis, another the Rotary Club, and the third the Lions Clubs. In addition many directors are very active in community groups, such as parks, library, school board, block clubs, and so forth. As such, you are expected to attend various social functions—banquets, award presentations, and so forth. Since this is not an elective but something that you are expected to attend, such affairs can be very demanding and detract from what little time you have with your family. But as noted earlier, such exposure goes with the territory and helps to keep you in front of the public eye. In some communities, funeral directors are known as joiners perhaps more so than almost any other occupational group. Finally, there are the professional activities that many, if not most, funeral directors are involved in. The largest of these, the National Funeral Directors Association (see Appendix A), sponsors an annual convention as well as seminars where various subjects, legislation, and new developments of interest to members are discussed. The association also publishes a monthly magazine, the *Director*, which is widely read within the industry.

The association estimates that more than two-thirds of the nation's funeral homes are represented among its membership. Other leading trade and professional associates in the industry also are listed.

CHAPTER 4

LICENSURE REQUIREMENTS

Licensure as a funeral director is a somewhat lengthy and involved procedure that requires that you be at least twenty-one, have some college background (the amount varies from state to state), attend mortuary college (here, again, the amount of schooling varies), complete an apprenticeship of one to two years (and in a very few cases, three years), and pass a national board examination.

In 1996 there were forty-two mortuary science schools accredited by the American Board of Funeral Service Education, the officially recognized accrediting agency by the U.S. Department of Education. You must have at least a 2.0 (C) average (the amount varies from school to school) to be admitted. In addition, most likely the school will require several letters of recommendation, a brief (500 words is customary) essay on why you want to attend mortuary college, and a personal interview.

In short since admission requirements for mortuary school do vary so much, it is important that you contact the school in which you are interested to obtain specific information on what they require. A list of schools accredited by the American Board of Funeral Service Education is contained in Appendix B.

These requirements help the school to judge how serious you are about pursuing an education leading to licensure as a funeral director. Many would-be mortuary school students have the mistaken perception that serving as a funeral director is lucrative, involves little manpower and time, and is easily accomplished And it is precisely this misconception that causes many students and graduates to leave the profession every year. That is why many schools take steps to ensure that the students that they accept will have the dedication and concern that is required to succeed in this career.

Make no mistake, the mortuary college curriculum is no snap. It ranges in length from one to three years, depending on the school. A few schools require that you complete four years of study and award a bachelor's degree at the end of your studies.

The program is especially intense in schools where it is only one year in length. A one-year school offers the big advantage of compressing the curriculum into one intense period of study. However, you may have to attend class year-round—you are in school every morning from 9:00 A.M. until 1:00 P.M. and then you work in a funeral home for the rest of the day until about 8:00 or 9:00 P.M. In what little spare time you have, chances are you will be studying, which leaves precious little time for your family, friends, or for recreation, sports, or hobbies.

It is quite common for out-of-state students to find housing in various local funeral homes. This not only enables you to take advantage of inexpensive housing, but it also allows you to get some practical experience as to what it is like to work in a funeral home and to earn a nominal wage at the same time, if you have had little or no previous background in this field.

Other students elect to live off campus in private apartments or to share an apartment, while still others find housing in private homes that have rooms for rent.

What does a typical mortuary school curriculum look like? Somewhat surprisingly, it includes many subjects that you would not associate with funeral service, such as business management and oral and written communications, and it is quite heavy in the sciences—pathology, anatomy, and chemistry. A typical program would include courses in the following categories:

- Public Health and Technical Areas: embalming, restorative art, chemistry, microbiology, pathology, and anatomy.
- Business Management Area: small business management, funeral home management and merchandising, accounting, computers in funeral service.
- Social Science Area: history of funeral service, sociology of funeral service, psychology of grief, grief counseling, oral and written communications.
- Legal, Ethical, and Regulatory Areas: funeral service law, business law, and ethics.

Tuition, though relatively inexpensive, is still a sizable sum of money if you are of limited means. It can range from a few thousand dollars a year to more than seven thousand dollars. Fortunately, financial assistance is available to the students who need it (estimated at about 35 percent of those attending). Typically many schools participate in two types of Title IV programs:

- The Pell Grant, which provides funds if you do not have the financial resources to attend college. You need not repay funds received from this program.
- Student loans, and many schools can provide several kinds of loans.

The Subsidized Stafford loan, which provides low-interest loans can be deferred until you have served your apprenticeship. The government pays the interest on this loan while you are attending college.

The Unsubsidized Stafford Loan, offered at a higher rate than the subsidized loan, is payable six months after graduation.

In addition many state and national funeral service organizations offer scholarships and grants for qualified students pursuing mortuary college education. A complete list of these scholarships is contained in Appendix D.

Besides the scholarships offered by the mortuary college or local and state funeral associations, there are literally hundreds of scholarships offered by charitably minded individuals, corporations, and foundations. Some of these scholarships, however, are restricted to students of a given nationality, religion, or race, or who live in a certain community or state. It may take a little legwork to uncover such aids, but the effort will be worthwhile since you may well qualify for one or more of them.

Once you complete mortuary college, you are eligible to take the Conference of Funeral Service Examining Board examination accepted by forty state boards in place of their own licensing examinations. The exam includes written and oral tests and requires that you provide a demonstration of practical skills.

Education out of the way, apprenticeship is the next hurdle that must be surmounted before you can be licensed as a funeral director. Here again the requirements vary from state to state, both as to the length of the apprenticeship (one year in most states, and two years in many others) and as to whether apprenticeship can be completed before or after mortuary school. In many states you have the option of completing your apprenticeship before or after mortuary school. Here again check with the agency listed in Appendix C for the specific educational and apprenticeship requirements for your state.

Apprenticeships, which must be completed under the supervision of an experienced and licensed funeral director, provide practical experience in all aspects of funeral service from embalming to transporting of the deceased.

As an apprentice you do a little of nearly everything. You might, for instance, assist in embalmings, in helping to cosmeticize the dead, in placing the dead in caskets, and in assisting during funerals. You might also drive a coach or the lead car or deliver flowers to area nursing homes after the services. In many smaller homes, where there is no porter or maintenance man, you might have to do a lot of the cleanup and maintenance work and wash hearses and other funeral cars. If there is to be a visitation the following day, you must make sure there is plenty of coffee on hand, and you may be assigned to receive visitors as they enter the funeral home, directing them to the area where the wake or visitation is being held.

In some states, as an apprentice you are expected to perform a given number of embalmings and funeral arrangements during the apprenticeship, be that a year or two years. In Illinois, for instance, you are expected to document that you have performed twenty-four embalmings and twenty-four funeral arrangements in one year. But here again this varies from state to state, and it is best to check with the authorized state agency listed in Appendix C for licensure of funeral directors.

Once you have passed the conference examination and completed your apprenticeship, you are eligible for licensure as a funeral director/embalmer in most states. Here again the requirements vary from state to state. In some the requirements arc different for licensure as an embalmer and as a funeral director. In others you must be licensed as both a funeral director and an embalmer. So here again it is advisable that you check with your state licensing board for the specific licensure requirements.

Once schooling is completed, the National Foundation of Funeral Service offers a continuing education program designed for those in active practice in the field. The three-week program includes classes in communications, counseling, and management. Since some states require that you meet certain continuing education requirements before your license can be renewed, it is advisable that you check with your state licensing board for the specific requirements in your area.

GETTING STARTED AND ADVANCING

Once licensed, getting started should be no obstacle. In many cases, apprenticeship is perhaps the best entree to making a connection for a job. Often the funeral home offering the apprenticeship does so with the understanding that if both the home and you establish a good working relationship, you will be offered a permanent job there.

Even if the apprenticeship should prove but temporary, the mortuary school that you attended should be able to help. In many cases, schools report placements of 90 to 95 percent of their graduates. Other opportunities are often uncovered at meetings of local, state, and national funeral service professional societies.

Once started, advancement is almost automatic if your job is covered by a union agreement. These agreements usually spell out what your salary will be as an apprentice and as a licensed funeral director, after stipulated lengths of service ranging from a year to five years. Such contracts also detail various benefits, participation in dental and medical programs, holidays, vacation periods, and much more.

In a large funeral home employing several funeral directors, there is always the possibility of advancing to chapel manager, where you help supervise the efforts of several funeral directors who report to you.

Finally, there is the possibility of purchasing or owning your own home. But in the large metropolitan areas, where most of the opportunities exist, this is getting to be more and more difficult for several reasons. For one there is the impact of some of the large funeral home conglomerates such as Service Corporation, Inc., and Loewen, which own thousands of funeral homes, cemeteries, and crematories coast to coast and overseas as well.

Because such large-scale funeral home operations are highly profitable, they can afford to pay higher prices for funeral homes that are on the market, and, therefore, can outbid you. As to building your own home, this is always a possibility, but in the metropolitan areas, this is a very expensive proposition, which can run anywhere from one to two million dollars or more. Today's funeral home is an extremely elaborate and often artistically luxurious operation. Unless you have accumulated a horde of cash, the cost of building is beyond the means of most would-be funeral home builders. But the possibilities of owning your own home are much better in the smaller communities, where many excellent opportunities are available. In many cases, if you lack the capital to purchase the home outright, you may be able to finance the purchase of the home with a bank.

So it is clear that the road to licensure and active practice as a funeral director can be a long and often cumbersome one. Is it worth it? You will be in a better position to make up your mind after you read Chapter 5, which discusses salaries and other supplementary benefits such as health insurance, pension programs, and vacations.

THE DEMOGRAPHICS OF FUNERAL SERVICE AND WHAT YOU EARN

What are the facts of funeral service as to size of the funeral home, population of the community the home services, number of homes operated, and number of funeral services performed each year? A recent survey of the National Funeral Directors Association provides the answers to these questions and to many more, including what you can expect to earn and fringe benefits.

DEMOGRAPHICS

For one, the survey showed that 44.8 percent of those who responded were from small towns or rural areas (population fewer than 10,000); while 26.9 percent were from small cities (10,000 to 50,000); 18.0 percent from moderate-size cities (50,000 to 500,000); and 10.2 percent from large cities (more than 500,000).

As to the number of services performed, 45 percent of the participants did fewer than 100 funeral services in 1994; 30.5 percent performed 100 to 199 funeral services; and 24.6 percent performed 200 or more services.

Other data included in the survey revealed that 91.1 percent of all funeral homes are independently owned and operated, and 80 percent are corporations. The study further showed that 83.3 percent of funeral homes are family operated, averaging forty-six years of operation by the same family. Individual owner/operators averaged 48.6 years of age.

The survey also showed that 65.4 percent of respondents operated only one home; about 20 percent operated two homes; and 14.9 percent operated two or more facilities. This does not, of course, include the large players in the funeral industry such as Service Corporation International, which in 1995 owned and operated nearly 2,800 funeral homes, 324 cemeteries, and 138 crematories worldwide, the vast bulk of these in the United States and Canada. SCI's funeral homes include some of the largest operators in the business.

Thus SCI owns and operates more than 10 percent of all of the funeral homes in the United States, a fact that must be taken into account in analyzing the number of facilities per owner or corporation and the number of funeral services performed. For example, one funeral operation in Chicago, which was recently acquired by SCI, performs more than 3,000 funeral services a year in its three chapels.

EARNINGS

There is little doubt that there is good money in funeral service, but considering the long hours that you have to work, the split shifts, the irregular hours where you might be on call one weekend out of two or three, and so forth, it is apparent that you work hard for every penny that you earn.

On that basis, the average salary for owner/managers, which accounts for the largest number of people employed in the industry, was $56,382, which was 9.3 percent higher than the average salary reported in 1994. The average bonus for owner/managers was $10,963, which brought total compensation to $67,345. But salary depends to a very large extent on the size of the funeral home and the number of services performed every year. Thus owner/managers of homes performing 200 or more funeral services a year carncd $77,751 a year; those who did only 100 to 200 services a year earned $57,758 a year; and those who did fewer than 100 services a year earned only $42,016 per year, plus the bonus.

The next highest paid job classification after owner/manager was that of mid-level manager, who averaged $40,169 in salary during 1994 and a bonus of $6,188. Those employed with large firms earned higher salaries than those at small firms. Those working at large firms, for instance, averaged $43,864 and those at small firms $32,386 a year.

The next most frequently reported position was funeral director/embalmer, with salaries averaging $31,250 in 1994.

Annual salaries for funeral director/embalmers in firms handling 100 to 199 services a year were $30,270; while those handling 200 or more services a year received $34,172; and those employed at the smallest firms, which handled fewer than 100 services a year, averaged only $26,410.

As to fringe benefits, the most widely reported benefit for 64.9 percent was a paid vacation. But here again size of the firm was definitely a factor, with only 8.6 percent of firms handling fewer than 50 services in 1994 providing a paid vacation while almost all (93.5 percent) of firms with 200 or more services a year provided a paid vacation for all of their employees.

Similarly only about 14.3 percent of the smaller firms, those handling fewer than 50 services a year, provided medical insurance; while nearly 90 percent of the larger firms, those performing 200 or more services, provided medical insurance.

Regardless of size, more than half of all firms provided a car to managers. This was as likely at small firms as at large ones.

As might be expected larger firms were much more likely to provide a pension plan for all employees. The survey showed that of those homes performing 199 or more services a year, 53.7 provided pension plans; while only 20.9 percent of those performing 50 to 99 funeral services a year provided their employees with pension plans.

It should be emphasized that these are national figures. Locally salaries for funeral directors, who are unionized in many of the larger cities, are considerably higher. Thus in Chicago, under a contract recently negotiated with Teamsters Local 727, which covers 245 member firms, a funeral director in his or her first year of licensure draws $755 a month; $774.50 in the second year of employment; $804 in the third year of employment; and $848.00 in the fourth year. From then on salary increases are intermittent and vary from one employer to another.

The above does not include vacation, paid holidays, overtime provisions, and health and welfare benefits. According to Mr. Thomas Pekras, Executive Director of Funeral Directors Services Association, which represents 275 funeral homes in Chicago and the surrounding area, the employer's contribution for health and welfare is $415 per month per employee and $225 per month for retirement pension. Such benefits added to the base salary would bring total annual cost per funeral director, in salary and benefits, to $50,000.

WORKING CONDITIONS

Working conditions in most funeral homes are excellent. Besides being clean, attractive places in which to work, most funeral homes are well lit and well ventilated.

Even so, as has been noted, funeral directors work long and irregular hours. Shift work is often involved since most funeral homes are open evenings and weekends. This means that when you're first starting out you may have to work several hours in the morning and then come back later to work that same evening. Also in many homes you will be on call to work weekends every second or third weekend. In the larger homes, where there are more funeral directors to share the load, you are more likely to avoid split shifts and weekends on call. But even so you are subject to the demands of the workload. Thus if several funerals are scheduled for the weekend, you may be called on for service even though you had not been scheduled for that period.

In addition to the long hours there is always the possibility that you will come into contact with a person who had a contagious disease, such as AIDS or hepatitis. However, the risks of being infected are almost nil if you follow proper precautions and are properly attired.

Also, to show proper respect and consideration for the families of the deceased, you must dress appropriately. Usually this calls for short, neat haircuts and trim beards, if any, for men, and suits, ties, and dresses of a conservative nature. This is not a field in which you are trying to call attention to yourself by the clothes you wear. On the contrary, it is what you say, not what you wear, that should be of prime importance.

Finally, you may be called on to lift bodies of considerable weight and to be outdoors in all kinds of weather—good and bad. So strength and good health are both called for in performing this kind of work.

CHAPTER 6

LOOKING TO THE FUTURE

On the whole the job outlook for funeral directors looks good for the foreseeable future. Employment opportunities are expected to be excellent with the number of openings for qualified mortuary college graduates far exceeding the supply.

Demand for funeral directors will rise with the increase in population and the corresponding rise in the number of deaths. The number of people aged fifty-five and over is expected to show a significant increase, at a rate much faster than that of the population as a whole. And deaths of younger people will show a rise due to the impact of AIDS, although it will not be as great an increase as in previous years.

While all of this is true, there are several trends in the funeral industry that can be expected to complicate demand in the not too distant future. For instance, cremations are expected to increase significantly. Currently cremations are seen only as a potentially significant threat to the traditional funeral service, accounting for approximately 18 percent of all funerals in 1992. They account for an estimated 50 percent of all funerals in California and as much as 70 percent in such communities as Sarasota, Florida. Still, in Indiana in 1992, cremations accounted for only 7 percent of all funerals.

In many cases, where the traditional funeral service and casket are done away with, as is true of most cremations, embalming is also dispensed with, thus lowering the cost of the funeral considerably. But cremation does not necessarily mean the end of the traditional funeral service because many families opt for these services plus the cremation, then placing the remains in an urn or in a tomb.

Today prepaid funerals are another distinct trend in the funeral industry. Only a few years ago, prepaid funerals represented about 17 percent of the funeral business; now they account for closer to 25 percent of all funerals, and they are expected to reach approximately a third of the business by the year 2000.

Prepaid funerals, in which you arrange for your own funeral and burial in advance, are, according to the experts, a means of achieving peace of mind. They help to ensure that your personal preferences are carried out, to relieve your survivors of financial distress, and to guarantee costs and establish spending limits.

Funds invested in prepaid funerals are put in interest-earning trust accounts and help to offset price increases in funeral homes. They are increasingly popular because the government subsidizes them. Since 1982 the government has targeted a portion of Supplemental Security Income payments for funerals. The states set their own spending limits on such plans, subject to federal approval.

At the same time there are unscrupulous operators in every industry, says Ernest Morgan in his book, *Dealing Creatively with Death.* He warns would-be funeral preplanners to investigate carefully all prepayment offers.

Another way to get around the high cost of funerals, currently averaging about $4,000, is to join one of the dozens of memorial and burial societies located all over the country. Forming considerable power blocs, such memorial societies are similar to buyers' cooperatives in that they trade in funerals instead of groceries. Typically they negotiate agreements with community funeral homes specifying the desired cost and the kind of disposal (burial or cremation).

According to John Blake, executive director of the Funeral and Memorial Societies of America, preplanned funerals from one of the memorial societies can save you up to 75 percent of the cost of the funeral.

But undoubtedly the most significant factor in funeral service, and the one expected to have the greatest impact in the near future, is the accelerated growth of such conglomerates as SCI and Loewen. SCI, out of Houston, Texas, currently owns and operates better than 2,800 funeral homes worldwide, including such well-known operations as Blake-Lamb and Piser Weinstein Menorah chapels in Chicago, McGilley's in Kansas City, and New York's venerable Frank E. Campbell and Riverside Memorial chapels. Loewen, operating out of British Columbia, owns an estimated 350 funeral homes in Canada and United States. Such huge conglomerates have become players to be reckoned with in the funeral service industry, controlling better than 10 percent of all funerals currently performed.

Extremely profitable, both SCI and Loewen emphasize cost economies in operation. Such chains need only one telephone operator to handle reservations and services for all the funeral homes they control. They also have a fleet of funeral cars available for serving any of their funeral homes, thus effecting considerable economies in the use of such vehicles. They have already seen considerable growth in the past decade, where SCI has grown from 662 homes in 39 states in 1992 to its present 2,800 homes worldwide. Through economies and more efficient use of their funeral directors and embalmers, they can manage more funeral services with fewer employees, thus acting somewhat as a brake on the anticipated growth of funeral directing opportunities in the near future.

So from the foregoing it is apparent that the future of the funeral service industry is somewhat cloudy, but it should be good for qualified graduates for at least the near future.

One thing is for certain, in a profession that traditionally has been male dominated, women are becoming much more of a factor. This is quickly apparent by looking at the increasing numbers of women coming out of the nation's mortuary schools. In 1991, 30 percent of the approximately 1,000 graduates were women. Fifteen years earlier, in 1976, only 8 percent of the graduates were women.

There is a good reason for this; many funeral home owners regard women as more empathetic with families at times of bereavement. As one funeral home owner put it: "They seem to be more sensitive to the needs of the family, and families can open up more to them at their time of grief." Women can be expected to be even more of a factor in the future.

Although all of the factors enumerated above will impact on the growth of the profession, some of them negatively, it is still anticipated that opportunities in funeral directing will see some growth in the years to come.

CHAPTER 7

CONVERSATIONS WITH THOSE IN THE PROFESSION

To get the perspective of those who are either in the profession or are contemplating entering it, we spoke to many professionals—students, apprentices, an educator, a funeral association manager, and several funeral directors. Some of those conversations are summarized in this chapter.

Apprentice Funeral Director

I am from Yankton, South Dakota, in the northeastern part of the state. And in South Dakota you need sixty hours of college credit in order to enroll in mortuary school, and it has to include a year of chemistry, a year of biology, and a year of anatomy. In Illinois you need thirty hours, but there are no specific requirements for courses that you have to take.

I went to the University of South Dakota in Vermillion for four years but didn't get my degree because I only took courses that were prerequisites for mortuary school and didn't have the other courses that were required for a degree.

I did my apprenticeship in South Dakota, but in order to meet Illinois requirements, I am going to school while serving another apprenticeship here.

I became involved in the funeral business because I have family connections in this field. And I would say that many of those entering funeral service do have some family involved in it.

I worked at my dad's funeral home in South Dakota one summer and ended up liking it. I then went to another funeral home, Miller Funeral Home in Sioux Falls, to get different experience and to make sure that I really wanted to do this.

That's the largest funeral home in South Dakota. They do about 850 calls a year. So we were really busy. It's the same here as it is in South Dakota as to the number of embalmings and funeral arrangements that are required to complete your apprenticeship.

In South Dakota you do twenty-five embalmings and five funeral arrangements at your own pace. In Illinois you do six embalmings and six funeral arrangements each quarter, which ensures that you are doing a good number of funerals each quarter and don't get caught short at the end of the year.

A lot of people entering this field are single. It's a very demanding job and can ruin family relationships.

There are several schools closer to my home in South Dakota, but I came here because of the school's reputation. The experience at Worsham is unexcelled. For instance, you go to the Cook County morgue once a week to do embalmings of the unclaimed bodies that arrive there.

It's a very intense course; there's no break. We go to school twelve months for the entire year. You get a lot of information, which prepares you well to take the conference exam that you must pass in order to be licensed as a funeral director. In Illinois you do your apprenticeship after mortuary school, and in South Dakota you can do this before or after mortuary school. But in South Dakota you must also pass a state exam in addition to the national conference exam.

The requirements vary from state to state for licensure. There are no national guidelines, which I think should be done.

Working with my dad on a one-to-one basis really helped me decide on this career. My brother is also in the business, and he still has a few months to go on his apprenticeship back home. And then he's going to go to mortuary school in Littleton, Colorado, since he wants to be closer to home than I am. I felt that it didn't matter. I wanted to go where the training would be the best.

Many schools have two-year mortuary science programs and award the associate's degree at the end of the two years.

As an apprentice you do a little of everything. A lot of the work consists of cleaning and building upkeep, and on weekends I wash the cars.

Another thing to consider is that you are pretty much on call all the time. You work long hours, which remains the same even when you become a funeral director. In South Dakota where I served my apprenticeship, I was at the funeral home on Christmas eve and on Christmas day. I did not get home because I was on call. It's very hard on the family because they do have to come second many times. I can remember growing up and my Dad having to leave birthday parties, Thanksgiving dinners, and so forth because if someone dies you have to be there for that family at that time. You can't put it off until tomorrow. They need you then. You have to leave whatever you were doing in five to ten minutes and get to the family and find out where the deceased is and make the removal.

As an apprentice I assist on embalmings, dress the bodies, cosmeticize and put makeup on them, place them in the casket, and assist in the funeral. I could be driving the coach or the lead car. I also help get set up for the funeral with flowers and afterwards deliver these to the nursing homes if the family wishes to do this. There's a lot of cleaning. In a funeral home of this size, they don't have a janitor, so a lot of this menial work is left to the apprentice.

If there's to be a visitation the next day, you make sure there's plenty of coffee.

You must pass the conference exam with at least a 75 to get your license.

In some states you must pass a state exam as well as the national conference exam before you can be licensed. Once licensed you do less menial work, but still some. In this funeral home the funeral directors help with some of the cleaning and maintenance work, but in Sioux Falls, which has a much bigger funeral home, they have a full-time maintenance man. There the funeral directors are primarily involved in arrangements and in embalming. Everything else the apprentices do.

In the larger homes the job is a more straightforward funeral directing job. But in smaller homes it's a mixture of some of the funeral arrangements and some of the maintenance and household chores.

Here they have about 250 calls a year, which is pretty average for most funeral homes. You do a little of everything. If you are on call on Friday, Saturday, or Sunday, if there's a death you will meet with the family and make the arrangements and do the embalming and make the removal.

First of all, you make the removal at the home, nursing home, hospital, or wherever, and bring the body back to the funeral home. Then you set a time for the family to come in and make the arrangements at their convenience. If they want an open visitation, you will embalm the body, and if they want cremation, the embalming is omitted. Usually you let the family have that night for making necessary phone calls, and the following morning they come in to make the arrangements.

The following morning when they arrive, you'll get the information for the obituary and the necessary social security documentation for pensions for the survivors. Then they'll decide on the casket, the vault, or if they want cremation, they'll choose an urn and the kind of service—if they want a religious service such as Catholic, Jewish, or Protestant. Embalming is not done as often in the larger cities. Here there's more of a trend toward cremation. But in South Dakota and in the Midwest in general, it's a lot more traditional and includes the full funeral, the casket, and the visitation. In our home we probably have 30 percent cremations and the rest traditional funeral, but that's only for the more affluent North Shore suburbs. The cost will depend on whether there will be a full service with the cremains or if there is just the cremation without the service.

Once you are licensed your income increases and there is a little less menial work. Students who live at the funeral home earn anywhere from $100 to $175 a week. An apprentice in Chicago will make from $18,000 to $23,000, and in South Dakota an apprentice makes about $12,000 a year, so it depends a lot on where you work and the size of the funeral home. A licensed funeral director will make anywhere from $18,000 to $22,000 in South Dakota during their first year. And in Chicago, a beginning funeral director will make on average the same as what a teacher earns.

Right now the number of funeral service students has increased a lot, much of it because of misconceptions of the work. In funeral service you pay your dues and work really hard and have long hours for perhaps twenty years. Right now my Dad's fifty, and he got into funeral service when he was only twenty-two. But he was very aggressive and wound up with four funeral homes. He literally worked his tail off. If you do have a chance to buy a funeral home, you have a chance to get an early retirement, but you must work very hard to build up that retirement.

You are on duty twenty-four hours a day, seven days a week, no holidays off. I can remember that from grade one to grade seven we took only four or five vacations, if that. Dad always had to be at the funeral home in case something happened, and we would run into situations where it was very hard for him to get away. I remember a time when were supposed to leave to visit my Mom's parents, and all of a sudden Dad got three calls and that was that—all our vacation plans went out the window.

People just don't die at your convenience from nine to five. Two nights ago we got a call at 11:00 P.M. I was already in bed and I had to get up and make the removal at the house that night and come back to the home to get ready for a cremation.

And you have to be able to handle the physical demands of the job, for instance, lifting a body to carry it to a hearse for removal to the home. If someone is killed in a bad accident, you have to be prepared to look at this person and then to place him or her on the embalming table and take care of whatever has to be done—like repairing any facial damage. I remember one case where a man walked into his house at 5:00 P.M. and shot himself to death with a twelve-gauge shotgun. You have to go to that house, face the wife and children, and do your work.

You should get involved to a certain extent—you have to. If you don't, I don't think you should be in this business. That's part of caring. But at the same time, you have to distance yourself because you've got a job to do. Eighty percent of the cases you are involved with are normal. But you are going to have to be able to look at all this kind of stuff without flinching. If you are on call and are just sitting down to Thanksgiving dinner and you get a call in the middle of dinner, you are going to have to leave. Larger homes are more flexible. You might have two or three directors on and two or three off on any given weekend, so you do get more of a break in the larger homes. But in a smaller home such as this, where there are only three funeral directors, one is off, one is on duty, and one is on call and can be paged if it gets extremely busy.

What I like about this business is dealing with the family and having them say afterward, "Thank you. I really appreciate all you have done for us." In funeral service you really create a bond with families that cannot be duplicated in any other business—doctors, lawyers, auto mechanics, and so forth. You see a person, but once you complete the job, you are done with them. But in funeral service, if someone's mother died and you see them two years later, you can say, "Hi there. How are you doing." They never forget you, and most of the time you don't forget them.

But people often get the misconception that you are always around the dead. They forget that most of our contact is with the living—the family and the survivors. The embalming part of the work will ordinarily take only hour or two. But the time you spend meeting with the family and the time of the actual service and afterwards, calling them up to make sure that all is well—that can run into dozens of hours.

With conglomerates like SCI gobbling up smaller independent homes, this is a trend I don't like to see because price is becoming a bigger factor in funeral service, whereas it has not been much of a factor in the past. People today are asking: "Am I getting my money's worth?" And this is resulting in the trend toward more cremations, which is going to change the entire shape of funeral service in the future. But you'd think with the larger corporations that they would help to drive prices down. But in reality their prices are higher and they operate on bigger profit margins. And you lose a little of the personal touch. In the family controlled funeral home, you think "this is my business"; whereas with SCI or Loewen, some of their homes operate on a nine to five basis. You've got different people coming in on shifts all of the time. So if someone dies at 4:00 P.M. and you get finished at 5:00 P.M., you'll probably leave that person for whomever comes on at 5:00 P.M. to handle. But in this funeral home, whoever is on that day would handle that call and remain on it until they were through.

Personally, I intend to move back home for at least a few years. Advancement depends on where you are working. If you are working in a family-operated funeral home, your chances for advancement are not as good as if you would be with SCI or Loewen. But in the family home, if you stay with them long enough, you probably will have a chance to buy the home, which is the ultimate goal of many funeral directors.

There's this perception that many in this business play a lot of golf and drive nice cars; but the nice cars are your business cars, and you drive them when you are running errands around town. Many people think that you are making scads of money. They look at the car that you are driving, but they don't realize that the pay is only average—it is not astronomical. At the home in South Dakota, where I did my apprenticeship, there was a funeral director who had been there since 1970 and who was making about $40,000 a year, but he also had full health coverage and they had a profit-sharing plan in which you share in the profits depending on how well the funeral home has done.

If you have no background in funeral service and are unsure of your suitability for this career, you should first approach the funeral director in your town about a summer job, if, for instance, you can help out around the home. If they don't offer you a job, go to the home anyhow and talk to the funeral director and see what they have to say about it. Just don't enroll in a mortuary school because you think it will be a neat career.

As to the embalming part of the work, if you are really dedicated, this should be no obstacle. In Missouri you can be an embalmer or a funeral director or you can be both, but this varies a lot from state to state. Restorative art pays very well, but you won't have a large clientele because a lot of people just won't want to pay that much money. For instance, a restorative artist is called in to work on the features of a person who has been killed in a bad auto accident. He could be working on this for more than ten hours at $145 an hour and this could really mount in cost. And most funeral homes do a certain amount of restorative work as well. Most funeral directors are trained for this to a certain extent.

On weekends in this home, the two funeral directors alternate in off time—Friday, Saturday, and Sunday. During the week the one with the least seniority works most evenings. In a smaller home, you just don't have the personnel to switch off. In my Dad's funeral home, for instance, he and my brother work together. So about all you can do is to try to plan to get away for a few days over a weekend and hope that it works out.

I know that there's a high burnout rate among funeral directors in the smaller communities for exactly this reason. In the early eighties, when my Dad was in his forties, he went through this and just took two years off. He sold all four of his funeral homes at the time and all he did was play golf. But once he turned fifty, he got the urge again and got right into it again and bought some more funeral homes. But that's not an option for everyone. In my Dad's case he started early enough to build up his equity in his homes, and when he sold them, he sold them outright. In the larger funeral homes, you have more flexibility and are not on call all of the time.

As to ownership, it depends on where you want to buy. In the North Shore area of Chicago, it would probably cost upwards of $1.5 million to build a funeral home. But in smaller communities in South Dakota, you can build one for much less, but it might be tougher to gain a toehold there since people are much more tradition bound and want to be buried where their father was buried and his father before him.

Also in funeral service you must keep a good public image. You can't be getting drunk and carousing around with women—that just doesn't work. That will kill a business like nothing else. People see you conducting yourself like this and they think, "If he's conducting himself like this in public, what will he be doing in the funeral home? We don't want someone like that to work on our loved ones."

And many funeral homes require that you belong to some sort of public service groups such as Lions, Shriners, Sertoma, and so forth, or they may leave it up to you, but it does help to become active in these various groups. I know that in South Dakota at the funeral home where I apprenticed, all of the directors belonged to a different club—Lions, Rotary, Kiwanis, or whatever. And various community groups as well, such as the park board, the school district, or church groups. It's good for a younger person who has the energy and drive, but it's hard on marriages. My parents are divorced, and I know that there's a high rate of divorce in funeral service. It's hard for a spouse to go along with the demands that pull you away from home all of the time.

It's hard to believe, but studies have shown that five years after going into funeral service, about 35 percent leave it, and that's primarily because of the misconceptions that I referred to above, that this work is easy and you make a lot of money at it.

Also women in funeral service is definitely on the increase. Being able to lift the bodies can be a problem sometimes. But on the other hand, women do well in funeral service because they have more of a nurturing attitude, and in many cases people will open up to women more than they do to men.

Mortuary School Student

Currently, I am a student, but as of September 1, I will be an apprentice. I grew up on the north side of Chicago and have had two careers before this. I'll be fifty in November.

When I finished college, I went into the office supplies and office furniture business, and later in 1982, I went into auto sales—my cousin owned a couple of auto dealerships. In February of 1995, I decided to go to mortuary school, and I've been working part-time in this funeral home while going to school.

I finished college in 1969 with a degree in math and psychology. I'm married and have two daughters, fifteen and eighteen, and the older one will be starting college in September.

I left the office furniture business after the company I was with went out of business. At the time, my cousin was just starting a car dealership and he knew that I was in sales, so I joined his sales staff. And after many years with him, my wife had been after me for a long time to get into a more stable profession—the auto industry is very up and down in sales and it involves long hours. This will have long hours also, but it won't be up and down.

I had been friends with one of the funeral home managers for quite some time and he had been after me to join them. Then when SCI bought our chapels, they needed some additional funeral directors, so he asked me to again join them. I visited him at this funeral home and I was here several times a week for several weeks to see if I would like it. It was at this time that I decided to get into funeral service.

SCI is the largest funeral service corporation in the world. They own roughly several thousand funeral homes worldwide and have just acquired 500 more in France; and they own cemeteries, vault companies, florists, and so forth, all related in some way to funeral service. They acquired our home, which is one of eight in Illinois and Florida, about a year ago.

What sold me on funeral service was the fact that I have always enjoyed working with people. I liked helping others and found that the funeral industry has had a bad rap just like the car sales industry because when *20/20* does a program on funeral service or anything else, they concentrate on the bad things. Yes, there are bad people in this industry as there are bad people in just about any other industry, but the good outweigh the bad by far. About 99.9 percent of those in the profession want to help you. And every service that I handle, I feel for the people involved.

As a student I attend school four days a week for six hours a day and take twelve courses each semester. It's very intense. You take everything from accounting to zoology. You must of course know embalming. About 20 to 30 percent of the students have family ties to funeral service. We have to know accounting and have to know anatomy—human or animal—and we have to know chemistry, primarily because it's required in order to be accredited in this state. The authorities want to know that you are getting a good general education, not only embalming and mortuary law. In the third and fourth quarters of school, on Thursdays we work at the Cook County morgue at the Robert Stein Institute of Forensic Pathology, where we do the embalming on all unclaimed bodies.

The program here is phenomenal. The teachers are unbelievable. Most of them have been here at least six to seven years. They gear everything to the profession, whether that be accounting, anatomy, chemistry, and we have to know the chemistry of formaldehyde, the hazards of it. At the end of the year, we take a national conference exam, which most states adhere to. To pass you must get at least a 75. Some states also require that you pass a state test—as for example, Michigan and Wisconsin. You also need at least thirty hours of college credit to enroll in mortuary school in this state. As I said before, it is really intense.

As for tuition, which is approximately $7,000, financial aids are available. My older daughter is going to college this fall, where the tuition is $17,000 a year. So while it may seem like a lot of money at the time, for the education you get, it's not.

Most out-of-state students will live at funeral homes in the area while attending school. We have two students living in each of our three chapels in the city. They answer the phones and work in the funeral home. We don't like to have people call and get an answering machine or answering service. It's much better to have somebody at the chapel twenty-four hours a day to answer the phone.

When they call at 3:00 A.M., a human being will be there to answer the phone.

I am in school from 8:00 A.M. to 2:00 P.M. Monday through Thursday, and from 3:00 P.M. to 9:00 P.M. Monday through Wednesday I work at the chapel and Thursday afternoon I am at the morgue. On Sunday I work all day, and we are closed on Saturday, since this is a Jewish chapel.

I did have some hobbies before enrolling in school and working here, but right now on Saturdays, I prefer to spend what little time I have with my family because when I get home after working all day until 9:00 P.M., I still have studying to do and I don't even see my family that much. So playing basketball or swimming and bowling have been pretty much curtailed.

We have more than 100 in the school and perhaps 30 percent are women; probably 90 percent are under thirty. There are only three my age. Last year, however, they graduated a student who was seventy-six, who had been a doctor—and perhaps even a lawyer—who was semiretired and wanted to do something else. This you can do even when you are eighty years old.

Here at the funeral home, I do whatever has to be done. There's an unbelievable amount of paperwork that goes into every funeral service. I just tried to get a hold of a rabbi and a cemetery. In a Jewish funeral, unlike other funerals where you might have visitation for two or three days, everything is rush rush. In a Jewish funeral, if someone dies on a Monday, the service will be held Tuesday or Wednesday, unless there are people from out of town who have to come in, so you have to coordinate with the rabbi, the hearse, the cemetery, the chapel personnel, and the chapel itself to make sure that it is free. If one service ends at 11:00 A.M., you have to see that there's Kleenex and fresh water. The student does that. I start work by typing a lot of material. Not too much is done by computer. We still type a clergy card and a funeral director's card. The family might want instructions on how to get to their home after the interment at the cemetery. We give the rabbi or any other clergy who are officiating a card with the name of the deceased; date of death; where they might be sitting the Jewish equivalent of visitation, which is held after the burial; where the cemetery is located; and the surviving members of the family. You can't expect a priest or rabbi to know every family they deal with.

As to funeral directing itself, we are not counselors. We suggest things that people can do. It's very hard for parents who have lost a child of three years, for instance, to cope with this loss. We will suggest certain counseling services that might be able to help them. But we are taught not give a lot of advice because we are not trained for that. We turn the counseling over to the counselors who are trained for that.

But we do visit kids in the high schools in the area—freshmen and sophomores—to give classes on death and dying. Surprisingly, the kids get a lot out of these classes. We know this from the kinds of questions they ask. You can't expect a youngster of fourteen or fifteen to know what happens at a funeral service. Because to tell you the truth, most adults don't know what to do when somebody dies.

When I finish school, I will be doing a year's apprenticeship in this chapel. I'll be working here eight hours a day and you do funeral directing. You meet with the families, you take the services out to the cemetery. You're more of a manager than a clerical worker. Right now, as students, we handle primarily the paperwork for the funeral director. We'll order the vaults, the cemetery plots, after the funeral director makes the arrangements. But as an apprentice you do the actual funeral directing. Once you are more than six months into the apprenticeship, you should be able to do the service without any supervision.

As an apprentice you have to do twenty-four embalmings and twenty-four funerals complete in this state. This must be documented with forms that you have to fill out and send to the state before you can be licensed.

In some states you can apprentice before you go to mortuary school. True that in some funeral homes you might hire someone to do embalmings, but in talking to other students, especially those from smaller firms, if you can't afford to pay someone $300 to $400 for an embalming, you do it yourself.

In the bigger cities, the work is more specialized. Some directors don't do embalmings. Some stick to arrangements and taking services out, whereas a couple of younger funeral directors who have been here only for a year or two will do funeral arrangements. If there is a need for embalming, they may have to do this. In our chapel, embalming is done elsewhere for all three of our chapels. Most chapels do their own and every chapel has to have a preparation room. We have one here, too.

In a Jewish funeral, they do not allow embalming or cremation, because it is believed that you go out of this world the same way you came in. You do not donate your organs to science either. But this is changing to the point where most families do accept embalming. It's not required except for certain illnesses, but aside from that, embalming is done to disinfect the body, to preserve it, and to restore it to a more lifelike appearance.

Ultimately, I would like to be chapel manager. If there are three funeral directors at a funeral home, perhaps one will be a chapel manager. I like the accounting as well as dealing with people. This is perfect if you like dealing with people and you feel good when the family comes and thanks you for doing a good job. The families are very vulnerable when they come here, and most don't have any idea of what to do when their loved ones die.

But like any other career, funeral directing has its negative side, too. We don't have nine to five jobs. We have to do a lot of PR, too. They don't have to go to our chapel—they could choose other chapels just as easily. So you belong to temple, B'nai B'rith, you go to dinners, you go to services, you have to know the rabbis and those who work at the temples. This has to be done so that you can be known to those in the community who might do business with you.

As to the future, I recently read a story in the newspaper that said that funeral directing was either number one or number two to get into. You have the baby boomers. It was felt that business will jump over the next ten years. But like any other business, there is competition. People will often shop around. We get many calls at our chapel from people whose loved one has passed away and they want to know what we charge. If they walk in and ask for a price, we must by law give them this information. There is a price list that itemizes all of the costs of the funeral service, such as if you want a chapel service, a graveside service, and they do send inspectors around. They will walk into a chapel and ask questions about prices, and if you don't give it to them, you could be fined $10,000.

As to cremations, among Jews they have been held only for about ten years or so in any number. Moneywise people know that cremation is the least expensive funeral, and in many cases they will choose this for that very reason. This is a growing concern because in many cases there will be no service at the chapel if there is a cremation. And this is a business, so you strive to have them choose a service at the chapel rather than a graveside service. And you want them to have a limousine and a nice casket.

As to my personal plans, I had a contract before I enrolled in school, but this is highly unusual. Perhaps 98 percent of the students don't have a job when they complete school, but the school will help you find a job.

As to earnings, funeral directors are unionized in the larger cities. As an apprentice you will make something like $450 a week. Upon licensure, you might earn $750 a week. In a year you might jump to $800 a week—everything is in writing and you know what you will be earning from day one. Our contract is with Teamsters Local 727 and includes benefits, too. But some of the benefits are just as good, if not better, working for our parent company, SCI. Their health insurance, vacations, and other benefits are just as good as those for the union funeral homes. SCI has a very good insurance program as well as a disability program.

As to jobs, yes, there are many openings. But getting situated in a particular home or in a particular area could be a problem. In many smaller communities, students often work in a home before coming to mortuary school, and they go back to their home town upon completing the program.

Many students are either family related or have had some experience working at a home, or at least they have been promised a job.

To know if funeral service is right for you, there are several things you should do. First, contact the school to get a better idea of the requirements, the courses, and so forth. And perhaps sit in on a class or two. We have people that do that all of the time.

Definitely contact the local funeral home. Talk to them and sit down with them. See what they go through and what funeral service is all about. I went to Indiana for a weekend and stopped by to say hello to the people at the local funeral home. They were as friendly as could be. They like meeting people in the industry and are more than happy to talk to you. As is true of any field, you may have great expectations, greater than what will actually happen.

So, know what you are getting into. Know that you really have to bend over backwards for a grieving family. That the family is in a very vulnerable position, and that you might have to do things that you might not normally want to do. You may have to be a referee. There will be squabbles within the family.

You have to know how to talk to the media. If you get a person who has been in the newspapers and who is famous, the media want to get involved. You may have to babysit the family. They may ask you to run over to so and so's house. "I know it's an hour away, but can you do it? We may not be able to get there." They may call you at 3:00 A.M. asking about this service or that one. You'll refer them to the funeral director who's on call for that night, and at 2:00 or 3:00 A.M., he or she will be talking to the family.

When you are a licensed funeral director, you might not work on a Sunday since that can be done by our apprentices and our younger funeral directors, but you're still on call nights during the week. You're still on call if it's a family that you've cared for before or who are friends of yours. You might have to come in on a Sunday to make an arrangement because they want you to handle it. You won't even try to palm this off on someone else.

For instance, if you are working at the Chicago chapel and there's a family in Skokie that wants you to do the arrangements, you would come to the Skokie chapel to handle the arrangements. You do whatever is easiest for the family.

Certain things are beyond our control. We don't control the cemetery charges for a service. We don't control what the newspaper chooses to include in an obituary. A death notice we pay for and control, but not an obit. And the family might think they are paying $6,000 for a funeral, not realizing that $2,000 is for the cost of the cemetery burial.

Mortuary School Student

I am handling advanced planning for this chapel and am also a mortuary school student. Prior to this year, I was working in the office products industry, and before that I was in advertising for about two years.

My father had been in hospice care and the hospice workers encouraged us to deal with issues that made death easier to deal

with, such as talking amongst ourselves and with my father about
death and how he felt about it. They also encouraged me to tell
him how much I loved him and to ask him if he was afraid of
death.

Shortly after he died, I met one of the funeral directors here and
we started talking and he asked me what I do for a living. And at
that point, following my Dad's death, I wanted to do something a
little more meaningful. I was grateful for what had been done for
us at the hospice, so I wanted to do something that could help even
one other family. So we started talking about the possibility of
doing this as a career. But I didn't really act upon this until almost
three years later. I was on maternity leave from my job and had
some time on my hands. I had planned on taking a number of
months off. And I started and went through training and obtained
my insurance license and began working with families in preplanning funerals for themselves and their loved ones. And I fell in
love with the work. That's how I decided to become a funeral
director.

I was doing this for a few months and was offered this position
as director of the department. I had also talked to the director
about the possibility of going to mortuary school. I felt at this time
a need and also the importance of being able to serve the families
that I had preplanned with once the death occurred. And I have
assisted at funerals. It's been a wonderful experience, as wonderful as death can be.

I'm in school Monday through Thursday and beyond. It's very
intense and I am grateful for that because I'd rather have more
knowledge than not enough. The staff is phenomenal. They are
incredibly supportive and provide us with so much information.
And a good percentage of the 100 or so students in my class are
women—about 35 to 40 percent.

As a woman, I have had some interesting experiences in funeral
directing. As far as the physical aspects of the job—such as lifting

a casket with an individual in it—that could be a problem, but that could be a problem for a man, too.

As far as attitudes are concerned, I have not run into anything negative in this chapel, but in class at school we have discussed this and most of the students are considerably younger—in their twenties. And this question of women funeral directors was posed to the children of funeral home owners, who were primarily men. If they had two candidates who were equally qualified for the job, one a man and the other a woman, which would they hire? They all said they would choose the man, primarily because of the physical challenges involved in the work. Again these students were mostly from smaller funeral homes where there might not have been enough people around. Fortunately, around here there are more than enough people to give me a hand if I need help or someone else needs a hand.

I've had nothing but positive experiences with families. In one case a woman who was attending the services at the graveside came over to me and told me,"I'm so glad to see a woman standing here." It touched my heart.

Primarily, I work with families that come into the chapel. I spend a very small amount of time learning the at need side— when the death has occurred. In fact, today I was out on a funeral, so it was a learning experience for me. But because my time is so limited due to school, I have to focus mainly on the advanced planning. I work about twenty-five hours a week at the chapel and about twenty-seven hours in the school.

Most of those in school are younger and don't have children or families, but there are a few people in my class in their fifties. There's no time when you can't make a career change in funeral directing.

I feel that I have a lot of life experience that can contribute in my work. But that's not to say that young people can't do very well and can't be sensitive to the needs of their clients. I have three children—eleven, seven, and two—and my husband is very supportive. I couldn't have done it without him. The advanced planning that I do has given me tremendous experience in making arrangements.

After school I have to do an apprenticeship and then decide if my focus will be in advanced planning or as a funeral director at need. I must decide soon. I am leaning toward the apprenticeship as a funeral director because that's my goal in school.

My apprenticeship will be at one of the three chapels that we own, but I am not sure which.

This work requires compassion. You must have lots of integrity and respect for both the dead and the living, and you have to understand that all this being so, this is still a business, too, and you have to try to fit all of this together, and at times it's tough.

It's tough when you're with a family and you want to be compassionate and you still have to ask them for the check at the end of the session. You have to be objective, but if you have a high level of respect and integrity for yourself and for others, everything else falls into place. It really does.

Sometimes arrangements can get very messy. It can happen because people have very definite ideas about death. Fortunately, that's the exception and not the rule.

As an apprentice, I am in the shadow of funeral directors, and I'm learning everything that I can, doing the embalmings and making arrangements and generally learning all of the details of the work—and learning about all of the paperwork involved so that you can have everything run smoothly from the moment the family walks in through the arrangements until we leave the cemetery.

There's a lot of detail involved and you must be very detail oriented. When you get out to the cemetery and before the casket is lowered into place, there's a nameplate on the vault. You've got to remember to make sure that you are in the correct place. It's the little details that you have to remember.

There are times when funeral directing can be very sad, and I go home and hug my kids. What I do in the advanced planning is not so bad. Occasionally, it can be if the death is imminent, but not ordinarily. I find it very sad because I get to know the mourners that I am making the prearrangements for, and when death occurs, it's more of a personal loss because I have gotten to know the family. It's easier to remain more objective if you never knew the family or the person who died. It's important to make the family feel that they have been well treated even though you may not see any of them for a long time.

I look for the business to grow through the year 2000 primarily because the baby boomers are getting older. And at some time, after my generation has died, this will affect the number of funerals, too. But that's not for a long time. Opportunities in funeral service abound partly because of people living longer lives.

As far as funeral service is concerned, the advanced planning and preplanning side is definitely worthwhile. And the goal is to watch that aspect of the business grow and grow, and the large companies are behind that policy and it will happen. So there's nothing but potential for someone seeking to get into funeral service.

Certainly the number of cremations are rising, even though this is contrary to the Jewish tradition, but even here it is rising, too. The West Coast has by far the most cremations; there are far fewer in the Midwest, which is more conservative.

Some people are extremely inquisitive and won't leave me alone for a minute when they find out my profession. One of my relatives won't even shake my hand. It varies, but mostly people are curious. I make it a point never to joke about my work. People may make a crack and I'll smile, but I never respond. This field is not a joke.

Mortuary School Student

I'm twenty-one and come from a small community near Peoria. I went to college for a year and got the required thirty-one hours of college at Central Illinois College.

When I decided on what I wanted to do for a career, in my junior year, knowing that several in my family are in the medical field—we have several doctors and nurses—I chose funeral directing. I really liked anatomy and the sciences as well as dealing with people. And I was in sociology class when someone said that there are a few things that will always be around—health care and funeral service. So I looked into the field and found it interesting. I had absolutely no relatives or friends in the business.

And I was involved in student council, which involved a lot of organizing and arranging of lessons. Everytime you are planning a funeral, you are organizing as well.

In mortuary school, I start hitting the books real hard two to three weeks before the finals start. Our class is probably comprised of students who are younger than those of previous years. Most of us are pretty young, except for two older students.

Many of the students have funeral backgrounds, but most don't. Of the forty-five students in my section, there are only about seven females.

When a person dies, nurses cannot take care of that person any more. It is left to the funeral director and embalmer to take over, and I take great pride in being able to care for someone's grandfather, which no one else can do at that time.

After school, I work in a funeral home in the city, which is also where I live. Some of the students have their own apartments or they share an apartment, but most of us live in funeral homes. After school, I arrive at the funeral home about 2:30 P.M. or so. If there is a wake, I'll get dressed and come down to do wake duty. Or, on a day like this where there is not much doing, I'll probably dress a body. And I will do some sign boards, which tell the names of the deceased and where the services will be held.

I will also do some of the minor cleaning—dust the floors and so forth. The work is at times overwhelming because I am supposed to be going to school, but there are other days when there's no work at all.

You get your board and it's kind of hard when your roommate asks you to go out and you have to stay home to answer the phones. I am on call twenty-four hours a day. I work until 3:25 P.M., and then I'm on call until I go to school the following day. We have to answer the phones and do whatever work needs doing.

My mother does organ donations in our town, so she does a lot of work in a similar area to what I intend to do. When I finish school in a few weeks, I have an apprenticeship lined up in my home town. So, I'll go back there to work an apprenticeship and hope that it leads to a permanent position, but I am not sure yet.

The father of the person who hired me said that he would never hire a woman. But when his father retired that's exactly what the son did when he hired me. And now his dad is eating his words and remarks on how well I've done.

My family thinks my decision to go into funeral service is just great, but I do take a lot of ribbing from friends. They are shocked and amazed when I tell them what I am doing. They recall that I used to participate in musicals, and somehow this just doesn't square with the image that they had of me. They associate funeral service with something that is sad, but it's not.

It's hard to say if this work is right for you or not. I honestly have a fear of death and dying, and this is my way of dealing with it, I guess. You have to come in contact with this work to see if you can handle it. Talk to funeral directors and perhaps they will let you observe the work.

Embalming is no problem since I had done some anatomy in college and it didn't bother me at all.

Mortuary School Student

I was in college before coming to mortuary school. In Illinois we need thirty credits of liberal arts and science to enroll in mortuary school.

When I was in elementary school, I decided that I was interested in funeral service. My dad's best friend owned a funeral home near where we lived and we used to go to a lot of wakes. This friend would always take me in the hearse every time we attended a wake, and he'd teach me about the business little by little. So, by the time I was in eighth grade and as a freshman in high school, I was really into it. I talked about funeral service all of the time.

I liked the fact that I was in the public eye and was the person that could best help people in their time of need. You were the last person that could do something for this person before they were laid to rest. It's a great feeling, and the way I look at it, if I didn't do it, who would?

Mortuary school is difficult. Many think that when they study here all they will learn about is mortuary science, funeral directing, and funeral arrangements, but it's basically a lot of science, and we study microbiology and anatomy and chemistry is hit very heavily. So you get some general studies as well as the mortuary science.

It's not an easy program. We work twelve hours straight through. In the afternoon, when school is over, I work for the funeral home that is owned by my friend's dad. I'm a full-time employee there and am guaranteed an apprenticeship there upon completion of my schooling and a job upon completion of my apprenticeship.

Right now after school, I work in the funeral home and assist the funeral director in every phase of the work. I do removal of bodies, I assist in some embalmings, and I help out on arrangements for the funeral and help to meet the families when they come for their visitation. In the morning, I assist the funeral directors, driving hearses, limousines, whatever. I also take care of a lot of the paperwork, making phone calls, calling in death notices, and ordering vaults, caskets, and prayer cards.

When I am an apprentice my duties will be pretty much the same, but I will have more leeway—I can do all of the work as long as there is a licensed director on the premises. Apprenticeship is a year in Illinois. During the apprenticeship you do case reports. You must document that you have done twenty-four embalmings and twenty-four arrangements over a year's time.

I love the work, but being on call can be rough. Not everyone can work nine to five, in this business especially. If you go to work for one of the corporations, you can have fairly regular hours, but it's hard to get a job with them because they don't hire apprentices. So you're limited to family-owned funeral homes to start with, and there you are on call twenty-four hours a day, seven days a week. You might be leaving the house to go out and then get paged and have to return to the home to work again. And this continues as long as you work for a private funeral home. I know of one guy in funeral service where I work who will be fifty this year, and he's on call twenty-four hours a day, seven days a week and has been for the past fourteen years.

Most of the students come from the states immediately surrounding the school in the Midwest. Before registering here I spoke to a lot of professionals and I got to see the prep room, and this school was highly recommended, so I came here.

If you have your thirty hours of college credit, this school is not hard to get into. You need two letters of recommendation and have to write a 500-word essay on why you want to be a funeral director. This gives them some evidence as to why you want to go into this field.

There are loans available if you need financial assistance. And many of the state and local professional societies have scholarships that are available to needy students.

My family tried their utmost to talk me out of it, but I thought about it all through high school and then in community college. When I was eighteen, I started working for a funeral home—this was full-time during the summer and part-time during the fall. Even though my parents saw that I was really serious about the profession, they wanted to make sure that I would not regret it later in life. They wanted to protect me to make sure that I would not regret it afterward. So I finished at this community college, and they finally granted my wish.

You do a little bit of everything, including maintenance and embalming. As to the pay, if you work in a union funeral home, you are guaranteed an increase in pay every year for the first five years. After that, it depends upon your employers.

I recommend that anyone thinking of entering this business should take science courses in college—microbiology, anatomy and chemistry—because if you have a firm grasp of these subjects even before coming here, it will make your workload a lot easier.

Licensed Funeral Director and Mortuary Student

I'm from St. Louis, where I have been serving as a funeral director for the past four and one-half years licensed in Missouri. I am currently attending mortuary school trying to fulfill the requirements for embalmer in both Illinois and Missouri.

So, I am attending mortuary school to qualify for my embalmer's license. In Missouri I worked for several funeral homes and attended Forest Park Community College to obtain my licensure as a funeral director—that was a two-year program.

I had exposure to the business through an uncle in South Carolina who owns a funeral home. And it has been an aspiration of mine to be in funeral service since I was a little kid.

I remember vividly playing with my cousins with the little Hot Wheels cars and lining them up in a funeral procession, so I would say that it was my ambition to be a funeral director for at least the past twenty-five years. I am presently twenty-nine and single.

To me funeral service is just that—service. Often people can look at it as a merchandising business, but the real heart of the business has to do with service that is rendered to families that call on you as the funeral director. To me the real love of the business comes from serving these families in the best way that I can.

I know that I can't replace the loved one that they lost and that's not what I am trying to do, but the real heart of the business has to do with the service that is rendered to the families that I serve. I feel that being a funeral director is the first part of the healing process and moving on with one's life. It's my job as funeral director to say to the family and those who attend the service—yes, this person lived and this is the kind of person that he or she was—and being there to help the family and the kids make the decisions that they have to make.

In Missouri the requirements for funeral director are that you have a high school diploma, that you apply for the test, and that you serve a six-month internship under a licensed funeral director. Then you appear before the state board to take a written exam on the state rules and regulations concerning the care and transportation of the deceased. After that you serve a six-month apprenticeship under a licensed embalmer where you give evidence of having performed twelve funeral arrangements to the state board. You then appear before the board again and take an oral examination, after which you are issued a license.

So it is a rather involved process, and rightly so, because in Missouri we have proportionately more funeral directors than embalmers. There are 4,000 funeral directors and about 2,000 embalmers.

I have aspirations of owning a funeral home, and to me if you are going to be in this business, you need to know both parts of it—funeral directing and embalming. I realize that embalming is but a part of funeral service, which requires at most 10 to 20 percent of the time that we spend on funerals with the family.

And in Illinois you must have both funeral directing and embalming experience before you can be licensed for funeral service. Some states require that you have two years of college and some only one year to enroll in mortuary school. A few require that you have three years of college and one or two require that you have a bachelor's degree before you attend mortuary school.

In Illinois you must have a year of college and a year of mortuary science and then you must complete a one-year apprenticeship for licensure.

Right now I am attending mortuary college to be licensed as an embalmer. I attend school in the morning and in the afternoon I work at the chapel as a student employee.

Duties at the funeral home as a student vary from home to home. Some students wash cars, and for those who come into the business with no exposure this helps them to see what funeral service is like. This is not a regular job where you punch a time card. Some days you might have two or three funerals to do and others you might not have any, but there are plenty of other things to do.

All states require that you have some sort of an apprenticeship, except Colorado. Since St. Louis is nearly on the state line between Illinois and Missouri, I want to be licensed to practice in both states.

I have a couple of leads for an apprenticeship. In this business it's not just what you know, but who you know, especially from the perspective of one who is black.

Get to know some of the funeral directors personally so that when you send in your resume, they will say, "Oh yes, I know so and so" when your name comes across their desk. I would absolutely make it your business to go out and meet the funeral directors in whatever area you plan to practice in. I would introduce myself and tell them that I'm going to school and I would appreciate your taking me under your wing and showing me what you are doing.

I expect that I will be working in a black funeral home—that's almost a certainty. But I do aspire to owning my own home and that's what keeps me going. Once I am finished with school and apprenticeship and I am licensed, I will be in a position to venture out on my own.

You have to have a real love for this business to succeed, and I don't mean the morbid part of it. I know that a lot of people are morbidly curious as to what goes on, but you must be genuinely sincere about serving people. This has to be something that you really want to do because it won't be easy.

Exposure to funeral service is a definite plus in your resume, but I wouldn't discourage anyone who is curious about this to try to qualify as a funeral director. I would suggest that if you have any questions about the business that you talk to the local funeral director—black or white—to find out what this business is all about.

Unfortunately there is a certain amount of segregation in the funeral industry, and it's a stroke of luck that I am where I am right now—working in a white funeral home. I was hired more or less out of necessity since there was need for someone who could do the job.

For someone who's black and really wants to be in the business, it's something that they should do by all means. But you will be tired. It will be difficult, but it will have its rewards if you persevere. For me there's no reward like realizing that I've done all that

I can for the bereaved and that they are satisfied with all that I've done.

Historically most of those going into funeral service are from families that have been in the business for many years—it has been a family-run business. But in the current time, we are seeing more black students in the mortuary colleges. In my school there are about six black students out of a student body of more than 100 students, and this is also true of the school that I attended in Missouri, where there were about 5 percent black students.

I am sure that it will be difficult to get situated as an apprentice, but after licensure it's primarily a matter of marketing, and I am sure that it will work out. There is a real demand for licensed funeral directors in the black community, but there are many currently employed in black funeral homes who are not licensed, and it's hard to stop this kind of abuse. I would suggest that if you are interested that you investigate the field thoroughly to see if this is what you really want.

Executive Director of a Local Funeral Directors Association

I did my undergraduate work at Lake Forest College, majoring in English, and taught language arts in elementary and junior high schools in Chicago and in Park Ridge for eleven years. And I have a master's degree in school administration from Loyola University.

I worked for the state board of education—then called the office of the Superintendent of Public Instruction—for six years. I was deputy director of postsecondary education in charge of visits to vocational schools and I administered the GI bill of rights. I also approved training sites for veterans, including state universities and community colleges as well as vocational schools and private colleges.

In 1977 I was appointed director of special audits with the state controller's office and was there for ten years. I regulated the licensing and auditing of funeral homes and cemeteries regarding trust funds and prearranged funerals for the funeral homes.

During the last seven years I was with the controller's office, the department was reorganized, and I retained responsibility for the regulation of funeral homes and cemeteries, and last year, in 1995, I was appointed executive director of this association.

Our organization represents about 275 funeral homes and livery operators in the Chicago area, which includes the surrounding counties and suburbs as well as Chicago.

We provide various services to members. One of our major responsibilities is for the management of the prearranged funeral trust. Currently we have some $25 million in this fund, and we invest it to try to get a better return for our members. When a person dies, the funeral home advises us of this and provides documentation of the death, and we in return send them a weekly check for whatever prearranged funerals they actually deliver on.

We estimate that 25 percent of the funerals our members currently handle are prearranged.

To me funeral service is an excellent career. There is the opportunity to own your own funeral home, which can be very lucrative. If you are an employee in the industry, wages are quite good in this area. Our members must belong to the union that represents our member funeral home's employees. And the contracts cover such things as wages, minimum wage requirements, and conditions. All of our member funeral homes are unionized, and we have negotiated contracts covering several classes of employees with the unions. We have two agreements with Teamsters Local 727—one for funeral directors and the other for drivers.

There have been many changes in funeral service over the years that makes operating a funeral home more difficult. There are a lot of federal, state, and local regulations that make operating a funeral home more costly. The Federal Trade Commission funeral rule went into effect in 1984 and was revised in 1994. Under this regulation funeral homes must disclose all costs involved in a funeral and must provide an itemized price list for anyone that comes in. Also the funeral home cannot make you purchase any items contingent upon the purchase of something else. You can't, for instance, force a family to have embalming unless they have a particular reason for it—be it for cosmetic purposes or preservation. The purchaser buys only what they want to buy, and they can choose what items they want.

Some of the funeral homes have gone out of business through mergers and acquisitions of such companies as SCI [Service Corporation International] and Loewen. There has been a marked change in customs and traditions. For instance, the number of cremations has increased perceptibly. When I first started in this industry in 1977 with the controller's office in Illinois, the cremation rate was about 9 percent. It has since more than doubled and currently is close to 20 percent in Illinois. California and Florida and the Northwest Pacific Coast are very high—in some cases up to 40 percent of the funerals in those areas.

Where formerly probably every funeral was traditional with interment, visitation, and so forth, now many cremations do away with this and are lower cost and less profitable for the funeral director. Cremation actually replaces interment as a means of disposing of the remains. And in this country at least in many cremations, memorialization, visitation, and church services are done away with in cremation. Very often people choose direct cremation where the body is removed from the place of death to the crematory for disposition. In some countries where cremation is very popular, such as in Scandinavian countries and in Japan, they do have a memorial service. The United States is about the only country where a large percentage of cremations do not include memorial services.

Also it's more common now to do direct burial—without funeral services at the funeral home or visitation. Very often the family may just have a short graveside service. If the family wants any kind of visitation, it's either at the church or at the graveside. Occasionally, they will use the funeral home for visitation, but most of the time they don't.

Large funeral home operators, such as SCI and Loewen, can effect cost savings by operating a number of funeral homes. SCI in this area currently owns and operates nearly forty funeral homes. This enables them to employ central embalming where they do all of the embalming in just a few chapels. These chapels do nothing but embalming, one after the other. And this does create cost savings and they can reduce costs in operation of funeral vehicles as well. SCI can afford to purchase their own vehicles instead of using outside livery vehicles, and they can share them among their various homes to get maximum use of each vehicle. And that way a hearse or a limousine can be utilized much more frequently. They can be used to service several funeral homes, and if a particular location has no funerals scheduled that day, they can be used elsewhere. They use fewer vehicles to service a large number of chapels.

But job opportunities are still good. We have an expanding population, especially in the suburbs and throughout the country. We're finding more women in funeral service and that's good. The women that I've had contact with in the industry are very good. There seems to be more of a tendency for women to be more compassionate and very sensitive to family needs. They are both cooperative and compassionate. I have attended the graduation ceremonies of the local mortuary school and have noticed a substantial number of graduates are female, where not too many years ago there were few women in the industry.

It's probably more difficult to own your own home nowadays, based on the increased involvement of the large chains, such as

SCI and Loewen, which can pay higher prices than you can. As a rule some of the chain operations can pay higher prices for funeral homes based on the savings they can effect and due to better marketing. And this in turn has raised the prices that funeral home owners can expect to get when they try to sell their funeral home.

Years ago funeral service was largely a family operation, and the children and grandchildren would carry on the business for generations. But at some point in time you reach the position where there is no offspring who wants to enter the business and eventually, they have to sell the funeral home. And often in these cases, the employees or a group of employees would pool their funds and purchase the home from the owner. Now it's more difficult because a company like SCI can come in and offer a lot more money than the employes can assemble. And to start your own home is very expensive. Today's funeral homes are more elaborate and beautiful, and costs can be higher than a million dollars and in many cases up to two million in this area to build your own home.

Employers are looking for funeral directors with good work habits, who are people oriented and who can work with people in a compassionate way since they deal with people at a time of crisis and need to be very sensitive to people's needs. Most families that come to the funeral director have not arranged a funeral before or at most have been involved in only one previously. It's not something you do regularly. If a parent were to buy a car for a child and the child just wanted any old car, if you bought that child the cheapest car, they would be happy. If they were expecting a Corvette, and you bought them a Ford Escort, they would be disappointed. Expectations mean a lot in this industry, particularly since the family is in emotional turmoil at the time. You must talk to the family and try to meet or surpass their expectations.

So we are looking for those who are willing to work hard and to make the kinds of sacrifices in time and effort that are called for. Funeral service is a 24-hour a day business, 365 days a year. People don't just die from eight to five. They can die any time. People expect that if the loved one dies in a home that removal will be made promptly and courteously. You can't treat the body harshly, and must be very careful with how you handle the dead person.

So while the impact of the large acquisition companies is still being felt, the opportunities are there, but it is harder to own your own home. Funeral directors are moved around from one funeral home to another and thus can operate with fewer people than someone who has to have someone at the funeral home all day even if no one calls. While it probably has cut the workforce some, the opportunities are still good.

As is true of medicine, the graduates tend to work in the larger cities, but there are many excellent opportunities in the smaller communities as well.

We encourage our membership for all funeral homes and would like to have a higher percentage of African owned homes as members, but one of the reasons they don't join is the union, which dictates salaries for wages, health and welfare, pension contributions, and so forth. Many of the African American funeral homes are nonunion.

Funeral directors in this state are required to have two years of continuing education, and this is required in many other states as well. Last year our association offered thirty-five programs equaling 100 hours for members and others in funeral service—a wide variety of programs from the technical to others such as compliance with the Controller's Act, FTC rules, OSHA regulations for health and safety, Americans with Disabilities Act, and others. This latter describes what funeral homes must do to accommodate those who are disabled in the way of bathrooms, ramps, and parking facilities.

Our primary function is to offer members services, which include several insurance programs with greatly reduced vehicle insurance and workman's compensation. We offer a trust program set up for funeral prearrangement plans where funeral directors can write an insurance policy with the money the family pays for such plans to cover the cost of the funeral. We offer a monthly newsletter and a hard-cover reference guide and diary, and we do some lobbying in the state legislature and help to resolve problems encountered by our members with state, local, and federal agencies.

We also provide certified copies of death certificates for families in connection with collecting social security benefits, Veterans insurance, and so forth. We work with the medical examiner's office and sponsor a variety of membership seminars on better business practices and more effective use of time, on regulations on the use of independent contractors rather than employees, and on how to better serve families in dealing with grief and stress.

Often the funeral director will enroll in a seminar and be unable to attend due to a funeral that they may have had to arrange. That's why we offer many more hours than the twelve to twenty-four hours that are required for continuing education.

We also sponsor tours where we go to other parts of the United States or abroad for continuing education. This year we went on a seven-day Caribbean cruise. Last year we went to Santa Fe, New Mexico, and before that to Vancouver. We also have some social functions, including a golf outing and a dinner dance.

We are very proud of our hard-cover book that we publish and send to all members every year. It includes a list of members, officers, cemeteries, hospitals in the area, and names, addresses, and phone numbers of area churches and synagogues. It also contains sections on licensing requirements and is updated and printed every year.

Other national organizations in funeral service include the National Select Morticians Group and the Order of the Golden Rule.

Those interested in funeral service must understand that the work is very hard. They must be prepared to work very long and irregular hours, weekends, and holidays. In many cases the spouses will do the primary parenting because the funeral director cannot always be there to help raise the children.

You may have to work nights. Some directors hire trade embalmers to do the embalming and to get some free time that way. But primarily they have to be ready to do this and such other duties as removals, arrangements, funeral services, some religious and nonreligious ceremonies, and to work with churches and cemeteries. Most funerals, church services, and burials are held during the morning—arrangements in the mornings and afternoons, visitations in the afternoon and evenings. Embalming is often done in the evening.

As an owner or manager of a funeral home, you probably would have to do all of this yourself, but this will depend on the size of the home. In a larger home, you get more specialization—some might enjoy the embalming aspect, others arrangements and working with the family, and some might use you for arrangements if you are good at that and in coordinating the various phases of the service. In the small firm, you are alone and must do it all yourself.

But the rewards are tremendous. If you do your job well, the families in most cases will be appreciative. Very often the family through word of mouth will tell another family of the great job that you did for them.

Usually funeral directors are pillars of their community, very active in community and service organizations and very highly regarded. Others hold them in high esteem as professionals.

According to the current contract with Teamsters Local 727, funeral directors in this area will earn $755 a week in their first year of licensure; $774.50 in their second year; $804 in the third year; and $848 in the fourth year. This does not include vacations, overtime, holiday pay, health and welfare benefits.

The employer's contribution for each employee is now $415 a month for health and welfare and $225 a month for pensions. It costs the funeral home approximately $50,000 a year to hire a full-time funeral director, including benefits.

Registrar of Mortuary Science College

The development of mortuary science education has followed the general pattern common to all professional fields. As funeral service expanded, research was directed to developing better techniques and practices that resulted in a rapid increase in the knowledge of the science. Today colleges of mortuary science are highly developed institutions of learning with curricula encompassing the natural and social sciences, liberal arts, and the specialized subjects indigenous to the funeral service profession.

Worsham College of Mortuary Science was founded by Professor Albert Worsham on March 17, 1911. From its inception, Professor Worsham placed great emphasis upon practical experience supported by scientific training from well-qualified professionals. As a result, Worsham College acquired, and continues to maintain, its status as one of the outstanding educational institutions in the country for the study of mortuary science.

Presently 145 students are enrolled, with the number of applicants increasing each year. Fortunately, the College has the capability to expand if the need should arise. I have been employed by the College for twenty-eight years. Approximately fifteen years ago, my husband and I acquired ownership; we were the most logical choice since we had been affiliated with the College for many years.

The student population of the College is very diverse in age and background. Thirty percent of the student population is composed of relatives of funeral service professionals. The remaining seventy percent have selected funeral service as a first career choice or as a change of career.

Applications for admission may be made at any time, however enrollments will commence only in March and September. Each student must supply the Registrar's Office with a completed application, an official college transcript (with a minimum of 2.0 required), a completed Health Certificate, two letters of recommendation, and a brief essay (five hundred words) describing the rationale for selecting funeral service as a profession. For those who need financial assistance, the Pell Grant, student loans, and scholarships are available.

The College conducts interviews of its prospective students prior to enrollment to ascertain the degree of experience they have had with the funeral service profession. The Director and I encourage students with little, or no, experience to volunteer time at their local funeral home—answering telephones and sitting visitations —in an effort to become more familiar with the profession.

Students intending to practice in the state of Illinois are required to obtain thirty semester hours of college, which should include a minimum of twenty hours of liberal arts and sciences and a maximum of ten hours of electives.

Students intending to practice in any other state must adhere to the regulations established by that state. A student may contact either the College or the state board for specific requirements regarding his or her state.

Students from outside the United States must supply the Registrar's Office with a translated transcript or statement from a recognized educational authority certifying that the applicant achieved formal education equivalent to a minimum of seven semester hours of college. Worsham College is the only North American college approved by the British Institute of Embalmers for the training of foreign students.

Worsham College does not provide on-campus housing, however the College does offer assistance in locating suitable facilities in three categories:

1. Funeral Homes. Many out-of-state students live in and are employed by local funeral homes in an effort to gain valuable experience. Thus they conserve on the cost of education and earn a nominal wage. Worsham College students have set a high standard of performance in the past and are eagerly sought by area employers.
2. Apartments. Some students elect to live in area apartments affording them more personal time while attending the College. The Registrar's Office maintains a list of students interested in sharing apartments.
3. Private Homes. The Center of Concern is an agency that pairs Worsham College students with clients in Wheeling and neighboring townships that have rooms for rent in their homes. This option offers the student the personal freedom of an apartment at a lower cost.

Upon graduation students write the Conference of Funeral Service Examining Boards, the licensing examination in forty states including Illinois. Students from Illinois must complete a twelve-month apprenticeship; during this time the student will submit twenty-four case reports to the Department of Professional Regulation for approval. Upon successful completion of both the apprenticeship and the Conference of Funeral Service Examining Boards, the apprentice becomes a fully licensed funeral service professional.

Worsham College is instrumental in assisting its students with job placement. Approximately 90–95 percent of our graduates acquire apprentice positions upon graduation. The College office informs the student population of those funeral homes seeking qualified professionals and offers assistance with resumes and cover letters. Salaries will depend to a certain extent upon demographics and caseload. Apprentices in rural areas earn approximately $19,000 per year with housing provided. Apprentices in urban areas, covered by the union contract, can expect a salary of $26,000 per year.

Funeral service is a rewarding profession with many opportunities. A funeral service professional must possess sensitivity and respect for the family as well as the deceased.

Funeral Home Manager

I am chapel manager of a large funeral home on the East Coast with several chapels in Boston and in Florida.

I have been involved in funeral service for the past fourteen years. Before that I was involved in marketing and sales promotion for several years and manager of a local radio station. I am a graduate of a local college and currently on the faculty of our mortuary school.

I am the fourth generation in the funeral business starting in the late 1800s with our first chapel in the city. Since then there have been several mergers, and most recently we were acquired by Service Corporation International last year.

I was in marketing and sales promotion since 1968 until I started here in 1978. Actually, I had some connection with the funeral business since childhood in several menial capacities, but I had not actually worked as a funeral director until 1978.

I had been thinking about going into the business for several years, and when the economy started dropping in the late seventies, I decided to make the change and to utilize my marketing and people skills in the funeral business.

I started as an apprentice, going to school at night for two years.

After finishing mortuary school, I contacted various funeral directors for an apprenticeship. This plays a very important part in learning funeral service—conducting funeral services, arranging and preparing for funeral services, and preparing the deceased for funeral service, which includes embalming.

For the most part people entering funeral service have a desire to serve humanity. Either they have had a priest, rabbi, or minister or a social worker leading them in this direction. The family background seems to be running out at least in our funeral homes. I am the last in my family to be involved in funeral services. None of my children want to continue in the business, and my sister who is involved in healthcare has no desire to join the family business. In fact I had no desire to become active in the business until I was thirty. So with my children not interested in continuing the family business, we need to reach out and find people other than family members who want to participate in family service. In talking to some of the younger funeral directors, it seems they have heard about this field through talking to others who were involved in the business.

They feel that while it's an honorable profession they are not going to get rich from funeral service. The hours are long and the work is immense.

To succeed, you cannot be selfish. You must be willing to dedicate yourself to meeting the goals, objectives, and wants of the client or family. You have to have the background to know from a legal standpoint what you can do and be able to understand what your facilities and manpower will allow you to do. For example, if you are involved in a big funeral service, you must know if you can provide the facilities or if you will have to arrange for this at the church or temple or whatever. You must also know if you can provide funeral service on short notice to make sure that you will have all the motor equipment you will need—the hearses and limousines. And you will have to provide the caskets, funeral merchandise, and be there for the family, whether this is 8:00 A.M. or 8:00 P.M. When someone calls, you have to be able to serve. You may have plans to go out of town and may have to give them up. If a family calls you, they are trusting that you will be able to walk them through their period of grief.

For the most part the hours are regular as any other office or business, but this is all subject to change with a phone call and you know this going in.

Once you have finished your apprenticeship and you are licensed as a funeral director/embalmer, the trick is to find a job. Job opportunities are good in the larger markets—Chicago and New York. There is not a tremendous turnover in funeral service. Once you find a job with a firm, you will generally stay with them for many years. Employer and employee loyalty is the rule.

Passing the state licensing test shows that you have the knowledge and experience to do the job. It is not too hard to pass if you have paid attention and acquired the necessary knowledge.

There are more opportunities in a metropolitan area. Because the Jewish community in Boston is small, there are a limited number of deaths per year, and this will support only a few firms. And because we have been so well established everyone knows us.

There are opportunities to own your own funeral home, but not in the metropolitan area. It is too expensive. There are only so many funerals and not enough to support more than one or two chapels in certain areas. If we did only twenty or thirty funerals a year, we'd have to go out of business, but in our three chapels alone in this metropolitan area, we do several thousand a year.

There are still many people who regard funeral directors as ugly, morbid people who wear black suits, and so forth. This has been the traditional image of the funeral director or undertaker over the years, but it is no longer the rule, if it ever was. No longer do you find the mortician rubbing his hands, in a high hat and horse drawn carriage. That's passé. With education, the funeral director is a public servant. We are trained professionals with a certain amount of psychological, business, and mortuary training that allows us to offer a family the help they need to get through this death process.

So we are now thought of more as a professional than as the guy in the back room with the dead body. The problem is that people don't always understand, and something that you do not understand or fear, you tend to make fun of. Sure, I get cracks all of the time. If I am at a meeting and my beeper goes off, someone will say: "Oh, oh, somebody just croaked." I just shrug it off. We are trying through education in grammar school, confirmation, bar mitzvah, whatever, to get over this fear and wrong conception of death and dying.

One thing is for sure, if you seek security and do a competent job for your employees and the families you serve, you can have a long-term relationship with the firm that you are affiliated with. Most of our employees have been with us for well over ten years—many have been here for more than twenty years.

I have more than eight funeral directors functioning in various capacities in this chapel. Several handle administrative tasks that need to be done—working out the cemetery arrangements, contacting the people who are to take part in the funeral service, ordering the casket, and so forth. They are involved behind the scenes rather than in direct hands-on work with the family.

If you are interested in funeral service, talk to your minister, priest, or rabbi. Talk to friends and dig down into your own life experience to see if service to mankind at what is perhaps the lowest time in a person's life is for you to see if you can handle the emotional and spiritual demands. You must have the right psychological mindset—that you are in business to serve others at a low ebb in their lives, and if you have done your work in school and paid attention in psychology and sociology classes . . . if you have the educational tools, you can draw on all of these to better answer questions and be versatile enough to help people at this time.

Funeral Director, Midwest

Our firm has been in business since 1901 and in this location since 1904. My grandfather started the business and my dad and my uncle took over when my grandfather died in 1933. I bought the business from my cousin who was running it until then, about eighteen years ago. But I have been working here in this funeral parlor since I was about fifteen.

This is about an average-size funeral home—bigger than some and smaller than others. Right now I have a full-time funeral director and a couple of part-timers.

About half of those in this business have gotten into it because of family ties or family connections. And others have gone into it because of the future that it offers.

I started as an assistant to the porter—helping to keep the place neat and tidy. I started from the ground up.

Embalming is still the preferred method of handling the deceased, but we do both embalming and cremation. Sometimes you will have a full visitation followed by cremation. And cremation is on the rise. The family may choose to keep the ashes in an urn, in a mausoleum, or take the urn home, or they may want to scatter the ashes over a given area, or over the ocean, and so forth.

We are nonsectarian and do all kinds of funerals. We don't turn anyone down for religious reasons.

What does it take to succeed? Well, for one you have to be ready to work. It's seven days week and it's twenty-four hours a day. People die at all times. They don't just die from nine to five. The work involves holidays and weekends and evenings as well. So you have to be very dedicated and able to cope with people when they are under stress.

I suggest that you get a part-time job in a funeral home to start with. You can't expect too much money to begin with—probably no more than the bare minimum. Possibly you will be working wakes—opening the door and greeting people and answering questions.

The Federal Trade Commission became involved in the funeral industry with regard to contracts and forms some fifteen years ago. It did so when some people were being taken advantage of by funeral directors. So the FTC mandated many regulations to help prevent abuses, and these regulations have been changing over the years. The government regulations determine how you derive your prices—not what your prices are, but how you get them. You have to have a price list itemizing each part of the funeral—visitation, hearses, casket, and so forth. It used to be that the consumer would be charged one overall price for the funeral depending on what casket they chose. Now you have to break this down into all of the parts, including embalming, use of motor cars, overhead for labor, and so forth.

After you graduate you must find a funeral home that will hire you as an apprentice. Some states will start the apprenticeship during your schooling or before schooling. In this state apprenticeship starts after your schooling. All of the schooling in the world will not mean a thing without some practical experience, and that's what the apprenticeship is for. The conference test follows your completion of school and apprenticeship. And then you are qualified to obtain your license.

This is a union area and all funeral homes in this area have a union contract that lists how much you earn as an apprentice, funeral director, chauffeur, and so forth. A fully licensed director will receive about $750 a week, after a few years experience. And this is plus benefits. Generally you work a forty-hour workweek, but you could work a split shift—so many hours in the morning and so many in the evening. Some students live in the funeral home or in living quarters nearby, which cuts living expenses considerably.

Job opportunities in this area have been declining in recent years due to mergers and consolidation, which has left fewer job opportunities. Some of the larger operations have been bought by some of the chain funeral home operators. Finding an apprentice position could be a problem in the city, but it's better in the surrounding suburban areas.

Owning your own home is not easy either because of the mega dollars involved. It's best to buy someone out—to purchase an existing, successful operation—rather than to try to start out from scratch. Perhaps you will work for someone and then after several years have the option to buy the funeral home when the owner retires. But you might have to spend of up to a million to start your own funeral home.

Many homes in the city are closing, but in the suburbs they are opening. A friend of mine opened up a home in the suburbs several years ago, and he's building another one right now. Through my association with various funeral homes, I have occasionally had to rent funeral facilities as required. It's always an option.

By working in a funeral home, you will learn the practical side of the business—the laws that are pertinent, the handling of various forms—the procedures for visitations, and the available professional services—and this must all be spelled out or you can be fined by the FTC.

Ordinarily we don't come into contact too much with really tragic deaths—accidents, killings, suicides, and so forth. You read about them, but don't come into contact with them very often. But when they do occur, you have to maintain your professional composure and must be equal to the challenge. You have to be able to cope no matter what the circumstances, even if it involves a tiny infant, for instance. If I get too emotionally involved, then I am not of much help to the family, and that's not what I am here for.

Sure, when people hear that you are a funeral director, they will often kid you, or think there's something strange about you. When I first started and was attending a cocktail party, for instance, and people would hear that I was a funeral director, somebody inevitably would have a question as to what being a funeral director is like. People are very unfamiliar with death and dying and they are very curious to know about the business, so I would take it all in stride and try to answer their questions to the fullest.

And you have to be careful about what you say. There are some people that you can kid around with and others that you can't. So you have to develop a certain sensitivity to your clients and what they want. You must be able to put yourself in their shoes—to do your best for them. You can be a great comfort in their time of need, and that's what it's all about. I've a drawer full of letters and notes of appreciation from people who absolutely on their own, voluntarily wrote because they appreciated the way that we handled their requirements. You can do a lot better monetarily in other careers, but there are many rewards that come with doing a good job.

While there is always some danger of infections, OSHA regulations tell you what you must do to protect workers, and so this is almost no problem. There are practices that you must follow to make sure that workers are properly dressed, such as wearing face shields and goggles, rubber gloves, and aprons. You must also have a drench shower on the premises so that should a worker be splattered by chemicals, you use the drench shower to wash off all traces of such chemicals before they get into your eyes or damage your skin. Drench showers came into being as a safeguard against the chemicals that we use in embalming, and you just pull the chain and you are under a shower about eight inches across. Such a shower must be tested to make sure that it is operative. This is done in the preparation room where all the embalming is done.

ADDITIONAL INFORMATION

ORGANIZATIONS

American Board of Funeral Service Education
13 Gurnet Road, Suite 316
P.O. Box 1305
Brunswick, ME 04011

American Cemeteries Association
3 Skyline Place, Suite 1111
5201 Leesburg Pike
Falls Church, VA 22041

Associated Funeral Directors, Intl.
P.O. Box 23023
St. Petersburg, FL 33742

Conference of Funeral Service Examining Boards
2404 Washington Boulevard, Suite 1000
Ogden, UT 84401

Cremation Association of North America
401 North Michigan Avenue
Chicago, IL 60611

Federated Funeral Directors of America
   1622 MacArthur Boulevard
   Springfield, IL 66274

Funeral and Memorial Societies of America
   6900 Lost Lake Road
   Egg Harbor, WI 54209

Jewish Funeral Directors of America
   399 East Seventy-second Street
   Suite 3F
   New York, NY 10021

National Foundation of Funeral Service
   2250 East Devon Avenue, Suite 250
   Des Plaines, IL 60018

National Funeral Directors Association
   11121 West Oklahoma Avenue
   Milwaukee, WI 53227-4096

National Funeral Directors & Morticians Association
   1800 East Linwood Boulevard
   Kansas City, MO 64107

National Selected Morticians
   5 Revere Drive, Suite 340
   Northbrook, IL 60062

BOOKS

Barrow, Edward. *Pyramid and Tomb.* Boulder, CO: Westview Press, 1975.

Boase, T. S. R. *Death in the Middle Ages.* New York: McGraw Hill Book Co., 1972.

Bowman, Leroy, Ph.D. *The American Funeral.* Westwood, CT: Greenwood Press, 1975.

Engram, Sara. *Mortal Matters: When a Loved One Dies.* Kansas City, MO: Andrews McMeel, 1990.

Grief and Mourning in Cross Cultural Perspective. New Haven, CT: HRAF Pr., 1976.

Huntington, Richard and Peter Metcalf. *Celebration of Death.* Cambridge: Cambridge University Press, 1979.

Lamm, Maurice. *The Jewish Way of Death and Mourning.* New York: Jonathan David Publishers, 1969.

Pine, Vanderlyn M. *The American Funeral Director.* New York: Irvington Publications, 1975.

Toynbee, J. M. C. *Death and Burial in the Roman World.* Ithaca, NY: Cornell University Press, 1971.

Turner, Ann Warren. *Houses for the Dead.* New York: David McKay Co., Inc., 1976.

Young, Gregory W. *The High Cost of Dying.* Buffalo, NY: Prometheus Books, 1994.

PERODICALS

American Funeral Director
Kates-Boylston Publications
1501 Broadway
New York, NY 10096

The Bulletin
National Selected Morticians
5 Revere Drive
Northbrook, IL 60062

Canadian Funeral Director
  Halet Publishing Ltd.
  174 Harwood Avenue, S.
  Suite 206
  Ajax, Ontario L1S 2H7 Canada

The Director
  National Funeral Directors Association
  1121 Oklahoma Avenue
  Box 27641
  Milwaukee, WI 53227-0641

Facts from the Foundation
  National Foundation of Funeral Service
  2250 East Devon Avenue
  Room 250
  Des Plaines, IL 60018

Funeral Service Insider
  Atcom Inc.
  1541 Morris Avenue
  Bronx, NY 10457-8702

Mortuary Management
  Berg Publications Inc.
  315 Silverlake Boulevard
  Los Angeles, CA 90026

Jewish Funeral Director
  Jewish Funeral Directors Association
  399 East Seventy-second Street
  Suite 3F
  New York, NY 10021

MAGAZINE AND NEWSPAPER ARTICLES

1. Grimsley, Kirstin Downey. "Jobs You Could Just Die for," *The Washington Post,* vol. 119, Feb. 8, 1996.

2. Goldman, Ari L. "For Funerals, a Female Touch," *The New York Times,* vol. 142, Feb. 13, 1993.

3. Pederson, Laura. "The Final Voyage: Giving the Public What It Wants," *The New York Times,* vol. 145, Oct. 29, 1995.

4. Presslcr, Margaret Webb. "Departings Not So Dearly Bought," *The Washington Post,* vol. 118, June 7, 1995.

5. Shermach, Kelly, "Pay Now, Die Later," *Marketing News,* vol. 28, Oct. 24, 1994.

6. Carlisle, Tamsin, "Loewen Returns to Takeover Path After Legal Woes," *The Wall Street Journal,* April 5, 1996.

7. Michaels, James W., "With Some Wry Amusement," *Forbes,* vol. 156, Sept. 11, 1995.

8. Ehrenfeld, Tom, "The Demise of Mom and Pop," *Inc.,* vol. 17, Jan. 1995.

9. Myerson, Allen R., "This Man Wants to Bury You," *New York Times,* vol. 142, Aug. 1, 1993.

10. Emling, Shelley, "It's Your Funeral: A Complete Consumer Guide," *Knight-Ridder/Tribune Business News,* Aug. 27, 1995.

11. Rowland, Mary, "Shedding Light on a Dark Subject," *The New York Times,* vol. 143, July 24, 1994.

12. "Undertaker Lives On," *MacLean's,* vol. 109, Feb. 12, 1996.

SCHOOLS OF MORTUARY SCIENCE

The following mortuary colleges and programs are accredited by the American Board of Funeral Service Education (ABFSE), an agency recognized by the United States Commissioner of Education as the official accreditation agency for mortuary colleges. ABFSE is located at 13 Gurnet Rd., Suite 316, PO Box 1305 Brunswick, ME 04011.

Alabama

Bishop State Community College
Department of Mortuary Science
 351 North Broad Street
 Mobile, AL 36603-5898
 Associate in Applied Science (2 years)

Jefferson State College
Funeral Service Education Program
 2601 Carson Road
 Birmingham, AL 35215
 Associate in Applied Science (2 years)

California

Cypress College
Mortuary Science Department
9200 Valley View Street
Cypress, CA 90630
Certificate (1 year)
Associate in Science (2 years)

San Francisco College of Mortuary Science
1598 Dolores Street
San Francisco, CA 94110
Diploma (1 year)
Associate in Arts (1 year)

Connecticut

Briarwood College
Department of Mortuary Science
2279 Mt. Vernon Road
Southington, CT 06489
Associate in Applied Science (2 years)

District of Columbia

University of District of Columbia
Van Ness Campus—Mortuary Science Department
4200 Connecticut Avenue, NW
MB4407
Washington, DC 20008
Associate in Applied Science (2 years)

Florida

Lynn University
Institute for Funeral Service Education
  3601 North Military Trail
  Boca Raton, FL 33431-9990
  Associate in Science (2 years)

Miami-Dade Community College
W.L. Philbrick School of Funeral Sciences
  11380 NW Twenty-seventh Avenue
  Miami, FL 33167
  Associate in Science (2 years)

St. Petersburg Junior College
Funeral Service Program
  P.O. Box 13489
  St. Petersburg, FL 33733-3489
  Associate of Science (2 years)

Georgia

Gupton-Jones College of Funeral Service
  5141 Snapfinger Woods Drive
  Decatur, GA 30035-4022
  Diploma (1 year)
  Associate of Science (2 years)

Illinois

Malcolm X College
Department of Mortuary Science
1900 West Van Buren Street
Chicago, IL 60612
Associate in Applied Science (2 years)

Southern Illinois University
Mortuary Science & Funeral Service Department
Carbondale, IL 62901
Associate in Applied Science (2 years)

Worsham College of Mortuary Science
495 Northgate Parkway
Wheeling, IL 60090-2646
Diploma (1 year)

Indiana

Mid-America College of Funeral Service
3111 Hamburg Pike
Jeffersonville, IN 47130
Diploma (1 year)
Associate in Applied Science (2 years)

Vincennes University
Funeral Service Education Program
1002 North First Street
Vincennes, IN 47591
Associate in Science (2 years)

Kansas

Kansas City Kansas Community College
Mortuary Science Department
7250 State Avenue
Kansas City, KS 66112
Certificate (16 months)
Associate in Applied Science (2 years)

Louisiana

Delgado Community College
Department of Funeral Service Education
City Park Campus
615 City Park Avenue
New Orleans, LA 70119-4399
Associate in Applied Science (2 years)

Maryland

Catonsville Community College
Mortuary Science Program
800 South Rolling Road
Catonsville, MD 21228
Certificate (15 months)
Associate in Applied Science (2 years)

Massachusetts

New England Institute of Funeral Service Education
Mount Ida College
   777 Dedham Street
   Newton Centre, MA 02159
   Mortuary Science Diploma (1 year)
   Associate of Science in Funeral Service (2 years)
   Bachelor Degrees (2 years beyond Associate Degree) in
      Bereavement Counselling and Funeral Home Management

Michigan

Wayne State University
Department of Mortuary Science
   627 West Alexandrine
   Detroit, MI 48201
   Bachelor of Science (4 years)

Minnesota

University of Minnesota
Program of Mortuary Science
   Box 740, UHMC, Harvard & East River Roads
   Minneapolis, MN 55455
   Bachelor of Science (4 years)

Mississippi

East Mississippi Community College
Funeral Service Education Department
Scooba MS 39358
Associate of Applied Science (2 years)

Northwest Mississippi Community College
Funeral Service Technology Program
8700 Northwest Drive
Desoto Center
Southhaven, MS 38671
Certificate (1 year)
Associate in Applied Science (2 years)

Missouri

St. Louis Community College at Forest Park—
Department of Funeral Service Education
5600 Oakland Avenue
St. Louis, MO 63110
Associate in Applied Science (2 years)

New Jersey

Mercer County Community College
Funeral Service Curriculum
1200 Old Trenton Road, P.O. Box B
Trenton, NJ 08690
Certificate (1 year)

New York

American Academy McAllister Institute of Funeral Service Inc.
450 West Fifty-sixth Street
New York, NY 10019
Diploma (1 year)
Associate in Occupational Studies (16 months)

Hudson Valley Community College
Mortuary Science Department
80 Vandenburgh Avenue
Troy, NY 12180
Associate in Applied Science (2 years)

Nassau Community College
Mortuary Science Department
1 Education Drive Building D 2085C
Garden City, NY 11530
Associate in Applied Science (2 years)

Simmons Institute of Funeral Service
1828 South Avenue
Syracuse, NY 13207
Associate in Applied Science (16 months)

State University of New York
College of Technology at Canton
Mortuary Science Program
Canton, NY 13617
Associate in Applied Science (2 years)

North Carolina

Fayetteville Technical Community College
Funeral Service Education Department
P.O. Box 35236
Fayetteville, NC 28303
Associate in Applied Science (2 years)

Ohio

Cincinnati College of Mortuary Science
Cohen Center
3860 Pacific Avenue
Cincinnati, OH 45207-1033
Associate in Applied Science (2 years)
Bachelor of Mortuary Science (3.25 years)

Oklahoma

University of Central Oklahoma
Department of Funeral Service Education
Edmond, OK 73034-0186
Certificate (2 years)
Bachelor of Science (4 years)

Oregon

Mt. Hood Community College
Department of Funeral Service Education
26000 SE Stark Street
Gresham, OR 97030
Associate in Funeral Service Education (2 years)

Pennsylvania

Northampton Community College
Department of Funeral Service Education
3835 Green Pond Road
Bethlehem, PA 18017
Associate in Applied Science (2 semesters or 2 years)

Pittsburgh Institute of Mortuary Science
5808 Baum Boulevard
Pittsburgh, PA 15206
Diploma (1 year)
Associate in Specialized Business (20 months)

Tennessee

John A. Gupton College
1616 Church Street
Nashville, TN 37203
Certificate (1 year)
Associate of Arts in Funeral Service (2 years)

Texas

Commonwealth Institute of Funeral Service
415 Barren Springs
Houston, TX 77090
Diploma (1 year)
Associate of Science in Funeral Service (16 months)

Dallas Institute of Funeral Service
3909 South Buckner Boulevard
Dallas, TX 75227
Diploma (1 year)
Associate in Applied Science (15 months)

San Antonio College
Department of Allied Health Technology
1300 San Pedro Avenue
San Antonio, TX 78212-4299
Associate in Applied Science in Mortuary Science (2 years)

Virginia

John Tyler Community College
Funeral Service Program
Chester, VA 23831
Associate in Applied Science (2 years)

Wisconsin

Milwaukee Area Technical College
Funeral Service Department
(West Campus)
1200 South Seventy-first Street
West Allis, WI 53214
Associate in Applied Science (2 years)

APPENDIX C

STATE FUNERAL SERVICE BOARDS AND LICENSING REQUIREMENTS

This information is subject to change without notice; students should contact their state board for specific requirements.*

Basic Educational Requirements

State	Type of License	Educational Requirements	Apprenticeship	State Board Address
Alabama	Funeral Director and/or Embalmer	High school and mortuary college	Two years before school	Board of Funeral Service 770 Washington Ave., Ste. 226 Montgomery, AL 36130
Alaska	Embalmer	Graduation from an accredited mortuary college	One year under licensed embalmer	Licensing Examiner Mortuary Science Section Department of Commerce and Economic Development P.O. Box 110806 Juneau, AK 99811-0806
	Funeral Director	30 semester hours from a college or university	One year under funeral director licensed in Alaska	

*Note: These are basic requirements only. Please contact the state board of your particular state for detailed information. An asterisk beside the state means the student must register with the state board before entering school.

Funeral director's license given to only one person per establishment. Other employees (embalmers or non-licensed employees) may do the duties of a funeral director under the funeral directors/establishment license. Main licensee is responsible for their actions.

State	Type of License	Educational Requirements	Apprenticeship	State Board Address
Arizona	Embalmer	High school and mortuary college	One year after school	State Board of Funeral Directors and Embalmers 1645 W. Jefferson Room 410 Phoenix, AZ 85007
	Funeral Director	High school and mortuary college, one year embalmer licensure and experience		
Arkansas	Embalmer	High school and mortuary college	One year before or after school	State Board of Embalmers P.O. Box 2673 Batesville, AR 72503-2673
	Funeral Director	High school	Two years, except with mortuary school, then one year before or after school	
California	Embalmer	High school and mortuary college	Two years before, during, or after school	Board of Funeral Directors and Embalmers 2535 Capitol Oaks Dr. Suite 300A Sacramento, CA 95833-2919
	Funeral Director	(Only business entities are licensed in this respect)		
Colorado	No current licensing requirements	Contact the Colorado FDA for information	Contact the Colorado FDA for information on voluntary certification	Funeral Service Board 7853 E. Arapahoe Ct. #2100 Englewood, CO 80112

State	Type of License	Educational Requirements	Apprenticeship	State Board Address
Connecticut	Embalmer and Funeral Director	High school plus associate degree in mortuary science (must pass the national board)	One year; get details from State Board	Embalmer/Funeral Director Licensure Dept. of Public Health 150 Washington St. Hartford, CT 06106
Delaware	Funeral Director	High school graduate. Two years of college (60 semester hours) and one year mortuary college (30 semester hours) Must pass national board exam	One year after school	Board of Funeral Service O'Neill Building P.O. Box 1401 Dover, DE 19903
District of Columbia	Funeral Service	High school and mortuary college	One year after school	Board of Funeral Directors Room 923, Occupational and Professional Licensing Administration 614 H St. N.W. Washington, DC 20001-7200
Florida	Funeral Director and/or Embalmer	High school and 12 month mortuary college program High school plus associate degree in mortuary science Must pass national board exam	One year after school	Board of Funeral Directors and Embalmers 1940 N. Monroe St. Suite 60 Tallahassee, FL 32399-0754

State	Type of License	Educational Requirements	Apprenticeship	State Board Address
Georgia	Funeral Director and/or Embalmer	High school plus mortuary college (12 months)	Two years before or after school	State Examining Boards 166 Pryor Street S.W. Atlanta, GA 30303
Hawaii	Embalmer, Undertaker or Funeral Director	Must meet one of three qualifications: one year of practical experience and graduation from a recognized school of embalming; or two years practical experience under registered embalmer in state and completion of four-year high school; or five years practical experience under registered embalmer.		Sanitation Branch Department of Health 591 Ala Moana Honolulu, HI 96813
Idaho	Mortician	Two years of college plus mortuary college	One year before or after school	Occupational Licensing Bureau Owyhee Plaza 1109 Main St., Ste.220 Boise, ID 83702
Illinois	Funeral Director and Embalmer	One year college plus mortuary college or associate or bachelor's degree in mortuary science	One year after school	Professional Services Section Department of Professional Regulation 320 W. Washington St. Springfield, IL 62786

State	Type of License	Educational Requirements	Apprenticeship	State Board Address
Indiana	Funeral Director and Embalmer	One year college plus mortuary college	One year after school	Indiana Funeral Service Board 1201 State Office Bldg. 100 North Senate Avenue Indianapolis, IN 46204
Iowa*	Funeral Director	Student must have a minimum of 60 semester hours as indicated on the transcript in a regionally accredited college or university with a minimum of a 2.0 or "C" grade point; and a course in mortuary science from a school accredited by the American Board of Funeral Service Education. The 60 semester hours shall not include any technical or vocational mortuary science courses.	One year after school	Iowa Board of Mortuary Science Iowa Department of Public Health— Lucas Building Des Moines, IA 50319-0075

State	Type of License	Educational Requirements	Apprenticeship	State Board Address
Kansas	Embalmer	Associate degree in mortuary science Must pass national board exam	One year after passing examination	Kansas State Board of Mortuary Arts 700 S.W. Jackson Suite 904 Topeka, KS 66603-3758
	Funeral Director	60 semester hours from a college or university (20 of which are defined by state board) Must pass state board exam	One year prior to taking board exam	
Kentucky	Funeral Director and/or Embalmer	High school plus mortuary college	Three years before or after school (mortuary college counts for one year)	State Board of Embalmers & Funeral Directors P.O. Box 324 Crestwood, KY 40014
Louisiana	Funeral Director	High school plus 30 semester hours college	One year apprenticeship, before or after school (contact board for details)	Louisiana State Board of Embalmers & Funeral Directors P.O. Box 8757 Metairie, LA 70011
	Embalmer	High school plus mortuary science program		
Maine	Funeral Director, Embalmer and Funeral Service Combination	One year of college plus mortuary college or associate degree	One year before or after school	Board of Funeral Service State House Station 35 Augusta, ME 04333
Maryland	Combination Funeral Director and Embalmer	Associate of arts in mortuary science	2,000 hours	State Board of Morticians Department of Health and Mental Hygiene 4201 Patterson Ave. Baltimore, MD 21215-2299

State	Type of License	Educational Requirements	Apprenticeship	State Board Address
Mass.	Funeral Director and Embalmer	High school plus mortuary college	Two years before or after school	Board of Funeral Service Leverett Saltonstall Bldg. 100 Cambridge St. Boston MA 02202
Michigan*	Mortuary Science License	Two years of college including 3 semester hours in public speaking/ communications, 6 semester hours in accounting, 6 semester hours in psychology/death and dying/ gerontology, 8 semester hours in chemistry lecture and lab, 6 semester hours in biological science, 6 semester hours in English composition/ business writing, and 3 semester hours in computer science plus one year of mortuary college	One year after completion of mortuary college requirement; contact state board for additional requirements	Michigan Department of Commerce Board of Examiners in Mortuary Science P.O. Box 30018 Lansing, MI 48909
Minnesota	Mortuary Science License	Two years of college plus mortuary college	One year after school	Mortuary Science Unit 121 E. 7th Pl. P.O. Box 64975 St. Paul, MN 55764-0975

State	Type of License	Educational Requirements	Apprenticeship	State Board Address
Mississippi	Funeral Service License	High school plus mortuary college	One year before or after school	Mississippi State Board of Funeral Service 1307 E. Fortification Jackson, MS 39202
	Funeral Director	High school or equivalent	Two years	
Missouri	Embalmer	High school plus one year mortuary college	One year	State Board of Embalmers and Funeral Directors P.O. Box 423 Jefferson City, MO 65102-0423
	Funeral Director	High school	One year plus one year internship	
Montana	Mortician's License	Two years of college plus mortuary college	One year after school	Board of Morticians P.O. Box 200513 Helena, MT 59620-0513
Nebraska*	Funeral Director and Embalmer	60 semester hours of college credit including 6 semester hours of English, 6 semester hours of accounting, 8 semester hours chemistry, 12 semester hours biological science relating to the human body, six semester hours psychology or counseling, plus mortuary college	Six months before and six months after or one year after mortuary school	Bureau of Examining Boards P.O. Box 95007 301 Centennial Mall South Lincoln, NE 68509

State	Type of License	Educational Requirements	Apprenticeship	State Board Address
Nevada	Embalmer	Two years of college plus mortuary college	One year before or after school	Board of Funeral Directors and Embalmers 305 N. Carson St., #201 Carson City, NV 89701
New Hampshire	Funeral Director and Embalmer	One year of college plus mortuary college	One year before or after school	Board of Registration of Funeral Directors and Embalmers Health & Welfare Building 6 Hazen Drive Concord, NH 03301-6527
New Jersey	Embalmer	Two years of college plus one year of mortuary college	Two years before or after school (one year credit for school)	State Board of Mortuary Science 1100 Raymond Blvd. Room 513 Newark, NJ 07102
	Funeral Director	Three years of academic college (non-professional studies)	One year before or after school	
New Mexico	Funeral Service License	Two years of college plus mortuary college (60 semester hours or 90 quarter hours)	One year	New Mexico State Board of Thanatopractice P.O. Box 25101 Santa Fe, NM 87504

State	Type of License	Educational Requirements	Apprenticeship	State Board Address
New York*	Funeral Director	One year of college plus mortuary college or high school plus associate degree in mortuary science	One year residency after school	Bureau of Funeral Directing New York State Department of Health Corning Tower, Empire State Plaza Albany, NY 12237-0681
North Carolina	Funeral Director and Embalmer Funeral Service License	High school plus 32 semester hours from, or be a graduate of a mortuary science college approved by the board	One year before or after school	State Board of Mortuary Science P.O. Box 27368 Raleigh, NC 27611-7368
North Dakota	Embalmer	Two years of college including 12 semester hours of communications, 15 hours of social sciences, 18 hours of natural sciences, 9 hours of business classes, 6 hours of electives, and mortuary college	One year after school	North Dakota Board of Embalmers P.O. Box 633 Devils Lake, ND 58301

State	Type of License	Educational Requirements	Apprenticeship	State Board Address
Ohio*	Embalmer	Two years of college plus mortuary college, including the following: 8 semester hours of science; 8 of English; 8 of Social Science; 6 of Fine/ Applied Arts.	One year after school	The Board of Embalmers and Funeral Directors of Ohio 77 S. High St., 16th Floor Columbus, OH 43266-0313
	Funeral Director	A person entering college from high school for the first time must obtain a bachelor's degree for the funeral director's license.		
Oklahoma	Funeral Director and/or Embalmer	Minimum of 60 college hours including completion of a degree in mortuary science, national board exam, Oklahoma State law exam, and oral exam. 60 hours may *not* be used to satisfy graduation	One year before, during or after school	State Board of Embalmers and Funeral Directors 4545 N. Lincoln Blvd. Suite 175 Oklahoma City, OK 73105

State	Type of License	Educational Requirements	Apprenticeship	State Board Address
Oregon	Funeral Practitioner	High school	Two years	State Mortuary and Cemetery Board
	Embalmer	High school plus mortuary college	One year	Portland State Office Bldg. 800 N.E. Oregon St., #21 Portland, OR 97232
Pennsylvania*	Funeral Director	Two years of college plus mortuary college. National board and state exam required for licensure	One year after school	State Board of Funeral Directors P.O. Box 2649 Harrisburg, PA 17105-2649
Rhode Island	Funeral Director and Embalmer	High school plus mortuary college	Two years before or after school	Division of Professional Regulation, Room 104 State Health Department Building 3 Capitol Hill Providence, RI 02908
South Carolina	Funeral Director and Embalmer	High school plus mortuary college	Two years before or after school	State Board of Funeral Service Department of Labor, Licensing & Regulation P.O. Box 11329 Columbia, SC 29211-1329
South Dakota	Funeral Service	Two years of college (minimum 60 semester hours of specific courses) plus mortuary college	One year before or after school in South Dakota	State Board of Funeral Service P.O. Box 1115 Pierre, SD 57501

State	Type of License	Educational Requirements	Apprenticeship	State Board Address
Tennessee	Embalmer	High school plus mortuary college	One year	State Board of Funeral Directors and Embalmers 500 James Robertson Pkwy. Nashville, TN 37243-1144
	Funeral Director	High school	Two years	
Texas	Funeral Director Embalmer	High school plus mortuary college Pass national examination and state law examination	One year after school	Texas Funeral Service Commission 8100 Cameron Rd. Suite 550 Austin, TX 78754-3896
Utah	Funeral Director and Embalmer	Associate degree in mortuary science from accredited school Must pass national and state board exams	One year before or after school	Department of Professional Licensing P.O. Box 45805 Salt Lake City, UT 84145-0805
Vermont	Embalmer	One year of college plus mortuary college	One year before or after school	State Board of Funeral Service Division of Licensing and Regulation Pavilion Building 109 State St. Montpelier, VT 05609-1106
	Funeral Director	Pass national exam		
Virginia	Funeral Service	High school plus mortuary college	Eighteen months before or after school	Dept. of Health Professions Board of Funeral Directors 6606 W. Broad St., 4th Floor Richmond, VA 23230

State	Type of License	Educational Requirements	Apprenticeship	State Board Address
Washington State	Embalmer	Two years of college plus mortuary college. The two years of college shall include one course in each of the following: psychology, mathematics, chemistry, and biology or zoology. Also, two courses in social science, three courses in English and three courses selected from the following: behavioral sciences, public speaking, counseling, business administration and first aid.	Two years training under a licensed embalmer in this state	Funeral and Cemetery Office—Business & Professions Divisions P.O. Box 9012 Olympia, WA 98507-9012
	Funeral Director	Two years of college (as above except for mortuary college)	One year training under a licensed funeral director	

State	Type of License	Educational Requirements	Apprenticeship	State Board Address
West Virginia*	Funeral Director and Embalmer	Associate degree from an accredited college or university or successful completion of not less than 60 semester hours or 90 quarter hours of academic work in an accredited college or university toward a baccalaureate degree with a declared major field of study, as evidenced by a transcript submitted for evaluation prior to beginning a one-year course of apprenticeship and prior to obtaining a diploma of graduation from a school of mortuary science	One year before or after school	Board of Embalmers & Funeral Directors 179 Summers Street Suite 305 Charleston, WV 25301

State	Type of License	Educational Requirements	Apprenticeship	State Board Address
Wisconsin	Funeral Director	Two years of college, including six semester hours of English and speech; 15 hours of natural science; 13 hours in business studies; 12 hours social science, 14 hours in electives plus mortuary college	One year before or after mortuary school; must have sophomore standing to apply for apprenticeship permit	Department of Regulation and Licensing Funeral Directors Examining Board P.O. Box 8935 Madison, WI 53708
Wyoming	Funeral Director Embalming	No educational requirements One year of college plus one year of mortuary college	No apprenticeship One year before or after schooling must be served in Wyoming	State Board of Embalming Barrett Building 2301 Central Avenue Cheyenne, WY 82002
Ontario, Canada	Funeral Director and Embalmer	High school plus mortuary college	One year after	Board of Funeral Services 415 Yonge St., Suite 1609 Toronto, Ontario Canada M5B 2E6

FUNERAL SERVICE SCHOLARSHIPS

The following list of scholarships available for funeral service students is not exhaustive, but provides some sources for funding. For more information regarding any of the scholarships listed here, please contact the appropriate source at the address given.

STATE FUNERAL DIRECTORS ASSOCIATIONS

Alabama Funeral Directors Association, Inc.
P.O. Box 56
Montgomery, AL 36101-0056

Two $1,000 scholarships. Applicant must be resident of state; monies paid directly to school.

Arizona Funeral Directors Association
6901 First Street
Scottsdale, AZ 85251-3414

$2,000 budgeted yearly; scholarships vary. Must be resident of state and maintain a B average. Monies paid directly to school in quarterly/semester installments.

Arkansas Funeral Directors Association
Penthouse Suite
1123 South University
Little Rock, AR 72204

Up to five $300–$1,200 scholarships per year. Applicant must be an Arkansas resident who has completed an internship at an accredited mortuary school, and agrees to work in Arkansas for at least two years after graduation.

Colorado Funeral Directors Association
7853 East Arapahoe Court #2100
Englewood, CO 80112

One $500 scholarship. Must be a resident of state; paid directly to the mortuary science school.

Connecticut Funeral Directors Association
350 Silas Deane Highway
Suite 202
Weathersfield, CT 06109

Up to two $500 scholarships. Must be a resident of state and enrolled in a mortuary science school.

Florida Funeral Directors Association
P.O. Box 6009
Tallahassee, FL 32314

Up to two each $1000, $750, and $500 scholarships presented twice a year. Must be a resident of state, student member of Florida Funeral Directors Association, completed 30 credit hours in an accredited mortuary science school with no "D" grade in any mortuary science required class, and have an overall grade point average of not less than 2.5.

Georgia Funeral Directors Association
44 Broad Street NW, Suite 208
Atlanta, GA 30303

Two $1,500 scholarships. Must be a Georgia citizen working in a member's funeral home, prove financial need, have funeral service experience, and letters of recommendation.

Idaho Funeral Service Association
c/o Mt. Hood Community College
26000 SE Stark Street
Gresham, OR 97030

One $500 scholarship. All inquiries are to be made directly to Mt. Hood. Scholarship information is not available through the association office.

Illinois Funeral Directors Association
215 South Grand Avenue West
Springfield, IL 62704

Two $750 and one $500 scholarships to each of the three Illinois schools totaling $6,000. Available to Illinois residents only.

Indiana Funeral Directors Association
1311 West Ninety-sixth Street, Suite 120
Indianapolis, IN 46260

One $500 and two $1,000 scholarships. Scholarship applicants must be residents of Indiana and intend to serve their internship in Indiana, and must be admitted to or already enrolled in a program of mortuary science education in an accredited mortuary science school.

Iowa Funeral Directors Association
2400 86th Street, Unit 22
Des Moines, IA 50322

Scholarship amounts are based on contributions to the Memorial Scholarship Fund and are administered through the National Foundation of Funeral Service. Must be a resident of Iowa and enrolled in an accredited mortuary science program.

Kansas Funeral Directors Association Foundation
1200 Kansas Avenue
Topeka, KS 66612

Two to four scholarships ranging between $250 and $1,000. Students must have at least one but not more than two semesters of mortuary science school remaining. Deadline: March 15

Funeral Directors Association of Kentucky
P.O. Box 1096
Frankfort, KY 40602

Scholarships vary. The student must work in Kentucky to receive the scholarship. Contact KFDA for further information.

Louisiana Funeral Directors Association
P.O. Box 8209
Clinton, LA 70722

Six to seven $750 scholarships. Must be a resident of Louisiana, submit application with all required information, and be examined by the Scholarship Committee.

Maine Funeral Directors Association
5 Wade Street
Augusta, ME 04330

One scholarship annually, varying amount. Scholarship goes only to second semester students; requires educational and personal references, school transcripts, and funeral statement.

Maryland State Funeral Directors Association
P.O. Box 1109
Lanham, MD 20703

Two $500 scholarships. Must be a Maryland student enrolled in an accredited mortuary science program with Maryland State FDA-member sponsorship and letter of recommendation. Taken into consideration will be financial need, academic performance, extracurricular and community activities, recommendations submitted, and articulateness of the application itself. Scholarships handled through the National Foundation of Funeral Service.

Michigan Funeral Directors Association
c/o Michigan Mortuary Science Foundation
P.O. Box 27158
Lansing, MI 48909

Three $2,000, $1,000, and $500 scholarships. Must write an essay and be a Michigan resident; financial need not necessary.

Minnesota Funeral Directors Association
300 South Highway 169, Suite 140
Minneapolis, MN 55426

One $1,000 scholarship. Applies to tuition only for the mortuary science program at the University of Minnesota payable in the first quarter of the senior year. Must be resident of Minnesota and submit high school and/or college transcripts, two essays, and letter(s) of recommendation.

Mississippi Funeral Directors Association
P.O. Box 7576
Jackson, MS 39284

One $500 scholarship. Must be a resident of Mississippi, a high school graduate, earned at least a "C" average in high school, and have evidence of need.

Missouri Funeral Directors Association
600 Ellis Boulevard, P.O. Box 104688
Jefferson City, MO 65110-4688

Four $750 scholarships. Must be a resident of Missouri and plan to work in Missouri following graduation.

Montana Funeral Directors Association
36 South Last Chance Gulch, Suite A
Helena, MT 59601

Two $500 scholarships. Must be referred by a Montana FDA member and plan to return to Montana to work.

Nebraska Funeral Directors Association
P.O. Box 2118
Hastings, NE 68902-2118

Minimum $1,000; number of scholarships given depends upon money available annually. Must be a graduate of a Nebraska high school, meet all premortuary school educational requirements of the Nebraska Bureau of Examining Boards, be recommended by a Nebraska FDA member, and be a resident of Nebraska.

New Hampshire Funeral Directors Association
62 Main Street
Pittsfield, NH 03263

Two $500 scholarships. Must be a student from New Hampshire and plan to return to work in New Hampshire.

New Jersey State Funeral Directors Association
P.O. Box L
Manasquan, NJ 08736

Two $1,000 scholarships. Applicants must be currently registered in a mortuary science program. Applications due by June 30th each year. Consideration based on academic performance and commitment to funeral service; financial need not the main determinant. Application process includes a written essay, copies of transcripts, letters of recommendation, and interview. Contact the state association for information on additional scholarships offered by local district associations.

New York State Funeral Directors Association, Inc.
3 Marcus Boulevard
Albany, NY 12205

Two $500 scholarships and one $300 scholarship. For the $500 scholarships, it is required the students be enrolled in a funeral service program at a New York State school.

North Carolina Funeral Directors Association
5860 Faringdon Place, Suite 2
Raleigh, NC 27609-3931

Over $400 scholarship. Also offer low-interest loans. Both limited to North Carolina residents. For $400 scholarship, must attend Fayetteville Technical Community College.

Ohio Funeral Directors Association
P.O. Box 21760
Columbus, OH 43221-0760

Eight to twelve $500–$2,500 scholarships (may vary). Offered to mortuary students who attend Cincinnati College of Mortuary Science or Pittsburgh Institute of Mortuary Science and plan to work in Ohio upon graduation.

Oklahoma Funeral Directors Association
6801 North Broadway #106
Oklahoma City, OK 73116

Up to $1,000 in scholarships (number of scholarships depends on need and number of applicants). Must practice in Oklahoma after licensure or monies must be repaid.

Oregon Funeral Directors Association
c/o Mt. Hood Community College
26000 S.E. Stark Street
Gresham, OR 97030

One $500 and one $1,000 scholarship. Must be enrolled as a full-time funeral service student at Mount Hood Community College, be a resident of Oregon or serving an apprenticeship in Oregon, prove financial need for aid, retain a 2.5 GPA for $500 scholarship or a 3.0 GPA for $1,000 scholarship. Scholarship monies must be used for tuition; requires a letter of recommendation from a school instructor or counselor.

Pennsylvania Funeral Directors Association
7441 Allentown Boulevard
Harrisburg, PA 17112-3609

Two $500 scholarships. Selection done by schools.

Texas Funeral Directors Association
1513 South IH-35
Austin, TX 78741

Six $250 scholarships (two a year to three schools). Must be a student attending a mortuary school in Texas.

Vermont Funeral Directors Association
One Rose Hill
Woodstock, VT 05091-1030

One $5,000 scholarship. Applicant must be an immediate family member of a member of the VFDA and a student attending a school for mortuary science; must be an employee of a member of the VFDA attending a school for mortuary science. Applicant must be a family member of a member of the VFDA and attending any college. Applicant can only receive a maximum of $1,000. Monies to be paid directly to the school at the beginning of the second semester. Applicant must maintain a 2.5 grade average.

Virginia Funeral Directors Association
5803 Staples Mill Road
Richmond, VA 23228-5427

One $500 scholarship. Must be a Virginia resident, be employed by a VFDA-member firm, prove financial need, have 2.0 GPA, and write a 200-word essay. May apply one year prior to entering college or if already enrolled and funds will be applied to second term.

Washington State Funeral Directors Association
2950 Northup Way, Suite 105
Bellevue, WA 98004

Scholarships available. Must be a Washington State resident. Please contact WSFDA for further information.

Wisconsin Funeral Directors Association
2300 North Mayfair Road, Suite 595
Wauwatosa, WI 53226-1508

Scholarships administered through the Wisconsin Funeral Directors Foundation.

Wyoming Funeral Directors Association
Box 1928
Rawlins, WY 82301

One $500 scholarship. Must be resident of Wyoming; monies paid directly to the school.

NATIONAL FUNERAL SERVICE ORGANIZATIONS

American Board of Funeral Service Education
P.O. Box 1305, #316
Brunswick, ME 04011

Fifty to sixty $250 and $500 scholarships available annually from various donor organizations. Administered by the ABFSE Scholarship Committee which meets in April and October. Donors may stipulate conditions under which their scholarships are to be awarded. Taken into careful consideration are financial need, academic performance, extracurricular and/or community activities, recommendations submitted, and articulateness of the scholarship application itself.

Conference of Funeral Service Examining Boards
2404 Washington Boulevard, Suite 1000
Ogden, UT 84401

Scholarships administered through the American Board of Funeral Service Education.

International Order of the Golden Rule
1000 Churchill Road
P.O. Box 3586
Springfield, IL 62708

Three scholarships with amounts depending upon monies contributed. Applicant must be a mortuary science major, in his/her final semester of study, maintained a B grade average in mortuary science courses, involved in school and community service activities, and must demonstrate excellence in the pursuit of knowledge in mortuary science.

National Foundation of Funeral Service
  2250 East Devon Avenue, Suite 250
  Des Plaines, IL 60018

No mortuary school scholarships available. NFFS does offer continuing education program scholarships for both licensed and nonlicensed funeral home staff.

National Funeral Directors & Morticians Association
  1615 St. Paul Street
  Baltimore, MD 21202

Scholarships vary. Recipients are chosen on the basis of their high school records, financial need and/or character and leadership abilities, and are selected by the Scholarship Committee. Applicants must be high school graduates and preferably worked in or had one year of apprenticeship. A basic course in chemistry and biology is preferred. Applicants must submit an NFDMA application form, two letters of recommendation (one from a sponsoring NFDMA member firm), resume, letter stating reason for request, and a copy of high school and/or college transcripts. All material must be received by Scholarship Committee 30 days prior to annual convention.

National Funeral Directors Association
  P.O. Box 27641
  Milwaukee, WI 53227

Scholarships administered through the American Board of Funeral Service Education.

MORTUARY COLLEGES

Cincinnati College of Mortuary Science
3860 Pacific Avenue
Cincinnati, OH 45207-1033

Ten to twelve $250–$300 scholarships.

Commonwealth Institute of Funeral Service
415 Barren Springs Drive
Houston, TX 77090

Eighteen $250 to $500 scholarships. Donors may stipulate conditions under which the awards are made. Applicants must be full time students at Commonwealth Institute with two quarters of satisfactory progress.

Dallas Institute of Funeral Service
309 South Buckner Boulevard
Dallas, TX 75227

Three or more $250–$300 scholarships. Must be in their third quarter of schooling at the Dallas Institute of Funeral Service.

Gupton-Jones College
5141 Snapfinger Woods Drive
Decatur, GA 30035-4022

Four $200–$500 scholarships. Richard Steward Scholarship: must be a Georgia student and have an A average; Ryan Cannedy Scholarship: must be a South Carolina student and submit a written essay; Rita Barber and Carolyte Vault scholarships: must submit a written essay.

Kansas City Kansas Community College
Mortuary Science Department
7250 State Avenue
Kansas City, KS 66112

Two $375–$400 scholarships (Gibson-Todd Scholarship). Student must be enrolled full-time in the mortuary science program at KCKCC.

Lynn University
3601 North Military Trail
Boca Raton, FL 33431

Varied number of scholarships offered for $480 each. Student must be currently attending Lynn University; scholarships available are for all majors—not specific to Mortuary Science.

Mercer County Community College
1200 Old Trenton Rd., P.O. Box B
Trenton, NJ 08690

One $500 scholarship and one to three determined by amount available from Alumni Association; and MCCC Foundation funds. Blanchard Scholarship is for students not eligible for financial aid from other sources. Financial aid available from several district funeral director associations.

Miami-Dade Community College
W.L. Philbrick School of Funeral Sciences
11380 NW 27 Avenue
Miami, FL 33167

Four $500, two $750, two $1,000 scholarships. Qualifications based on scholarship and need.

Mount Hood Community College
26000 S.E. Stark Street
Gresham, OR 97030

One $500 scholarship. Must be an Idaho student; scholarship recipient is selected by Mount Hood Committee.

New England Institute of Applied Arts and Sciences at Mount Ida College
777 Dedham Street
Newton Centre, MA 02159

Four $2,000 and one full-year room and board scholarships. Applicant must have applied and been accepted to the Institute to apply for a scholarship. Returning students are also eligible to apply. Good academic standing is an important criterion.

Northampton Community College
Department of Funeral Service Education
3835 Green Pond Road
Bethlehem, PA 18017

One $300–$500 scholarship. For scholarship, applicant must have a 3.0 GPA and be a full-time funeral service education student. Contact department chairperson for further information.

Pittsburgh Institute of Mortuary Science
5808 Baum Boulevard
Pittsburgh, PA 15206-3706

Scholarships vary, currently $1,000 each. Must currently be a student at Pittsburgh Institute.

St. Louis Community College at Forest Park
5600 Oakland Avenue
St. Louis, MO 63110

At least one scholarship for $750. Must be a Missouri resident who plans on being licensed in Missouri following graduation.

St. Petersburg Junior College
P.O. Box 13489
St. Petersburg, FL 33733

One $250 scholarship. Based on academics and need.

San Antonio College
Mortuary Science Program
1300 San Pedro Avenue
San Antonio, TX 78212–4299

Two full tuition and fees scholarships per semester. Available to Texas residents only.

Simmons Institute of Funeral Service
1828 South Avenue
Syracuse, NY 13207

Two $500 scholarships, one spring and one fall. Funds restricted to Simmons students. Contact the Institute for other available scholarships.

Southern Illinois University at Carbondale
College of Technical Careers—MC6615
Mortuary Science and Funeral Service
Carbondale, IL 62901

Thirteen $250–$750 scholarships. Students must be enrolled full-time in the mortuary science program at SIUC. All but one scholarship from the IFDA are restricted to students in the second year sequence who are in good standing academically.

State University of New York College of Technology at Canton
Mortuary Science Program
  Canton, NY 13617

Many scholarships available to SUNY at Canton students only. Contact College Foundation for further information.

University of Central Oklahoma
  Edmond, OK 73034-0186

Seven $250–$400 scholarships. Students must be enrolled in the funeral service program at the University of Central Oklahoma.

Wayne State University
Department of Mortuary Science
  627 West Alexandrine
  Detroit, MI 48201

One $500 scholarship. Applicants must have completed one semester within the mortuary science department and have achieved a minimum 3.3 GPA. Recipients will be selected by the Wayne State Office of Scholarships and Financial Aid.